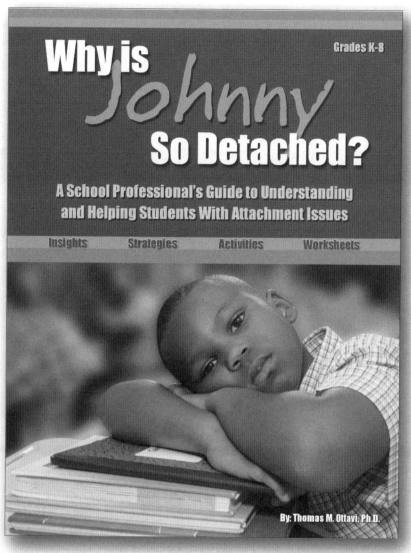

Grades K-8

Why is *Johnny* So Detached?

A School Professional's Guide to Understanding and Helping Students With Attachment Issues

Insights   Strategies   Activities   Worksheets

By: Thomas M. Ottavi, Ph.D.

© 2007 by YouthLight, Inc.
Chapin, SC 29036

Cover Design by Amy Rule
Internal Layout by Rebecca Gray
Edited by Susan Bowman

ISBN: 978-1-59850-015-8

Library of Congress Control Number: 2006939200

10 9 8 7 6 5 4 3 2 1
Printed in the United States

youth light inc.

PO Box 115 • Chapin, SC 29036
(800) 209-9774 • (803)345-1070 • Fax (803)345-0888
yl@youthlightbooks.com • www.youthlightbooks.com

Dedication

Why Is Johnny So Detached? A School Professional's Guide to Understanding and Helping Students With Attachment Issues is dedicated to youth everywhere working to overcome painful life events. It is also dedicated to the caring and committed parents and school professionals working with these children and helping advance talents, skills, and enjoyment of life.

Acknowledgements

I would like to thank Susan and Bob Bowman for their support and the opportunity to create this work. I would also like to thank my wife Patty and children Nolan, Casey, and Aidan for their support and support for education, life long learning and faith in God. Thanks and gratitude for all Ottavi and Schuster family mentoring and support for education and life long learning. Also thanks for professional support and feedback on these materials to: Phyllis Rubin, Sandy Ragona, Jon Filitti, Louise and Joe Ottavi, Diane Berg, Rose Meisch, Stefanie Weber, and Theresa Prier. Also acknowledgements for Hillcrest school professionals Cindy Olsen, Donna Bardon and all the many associates over the years for their dedicated and inspirational work done with students.

Table of Contents

Introduction

The Importance of Attachment For Development

Current neuroscience supports the importance of early attachment relationships for biological, psychological, and social development from childhood through adulthood (Seigel & Hartzell, 2003; Hesse et. al. 2003). In the psychological domain, healthy early attachment relationships establish the base abilities to trust, feel secure and safe, feel connected with our emotional states, and also the emotional states of others. Attachment relationships are instrumental for the healthy growth of the developing brain and are the anchor points for memory, personal story, and emotion and mental representations (Siegel, 2003). Persons with more stable and secure attachment relationships tend toward emotional resilience while significant disturbances in attachment or traumatic events often leads to poor adjustment. Poor and disrupted attachment with the addition of abusive or neglectful environments can create a lasting base of strong negative interaction patterns, poor arousal and emotional regulation, and a variety of basic coping deficits (Siegel, 2003). In the social domain, attachment relationships contribute to the basis for secure relationships that lead to seeing self and others with more accurate perception, using more effective communication, connecting thoughts and feelings, and viewing close relationships as important and meaningful. With the attachment process being so fundamentally vital for development, it is not surprising that when major disruptions occur in the form of neglect, abuse, or a prolonged chaotic home environments that the effects can be broad and significant.

Detachment from Family

Today school professionals are finding more children coming to school with histories of early childhood neglect, abuse, and relationship instability that significantly impact their emotional, social, learning, and behavioral development. Students come with varying degrees of past home disruption, placements in foster care, relative placements, adoptive homes, residential placements or emergency shelter placements. These disruptions almost invariably lead to experiences of acute stress (Chaffin, et. al. 2006) and a disconnection or detachment from many of the positive elements that schools can offer. Nationally, 523,000 youth spent time in foster care in 2003 (Child Welfare, 2005) and national statistics show over 2 million youth in the single year of 2004 were victims of child maltreatment with the majority of those cases being multiple forms of abuse (US Government, 2004). Schools inevitably receive students with a broad range of symptoms, traits, and impairment levels of attachment related problems and some attachment disorders. While some students are resilient and not overly affected, many students fluctuate in their ability to function in a school setting or make educational progress given the frequency and intensity of problems.

Attachment Diagnosis and Descriptions Issues

In *Why Is Johnny So Detached? A School Professional's Guide to Understanding and Helping Students With Attachment Issues*, we are not considering basic issues of daydreaming, common dislike of school or mild frustrations with having needs met at school. Rather, we are looking at students with childhood histories that have repeated disruption and painful life events creating gaps in their ability to consistently connect with the age appropriate roles and expectations in the school setting. A broader and more inclusive definition of attachment issues is used for this book: children whose behavior is affected by lack of a primary attachment figure, a seriously unhealthy attachment relationship with a primary caregiver, or a disrupted attachment relationship (Chaffin et al. 2006) and hurtful life events falling outside the typical range of experience for a child causing disturbances in behavioral and psychological functioning (van der Kolk, 2003).

There are disagreements in the field of clinical psychology about the exact definitions of attachment disorder and Reactive Attachment Disorder (RAD) as defined in the American Psychiatric Association's DSM-IV-TR. The RAD diagnostic category has been considered unclear, poorly studied, and viewed differently from within the fields of attachment theory, research, and clinical practice (Chaffin et al, 2006). The American Psychiatric Association's DSM-IV-TR has defined RAD as a markedly disturbed and developmentally inappropriate social relatedness in most contexts, beginning before age 5 years, as evidenced by either (1) persistent failure to initiate or respond in a developmentally appropriate fashion to most social interactions (excessively inhibited, hypervigilant, or ambivalent and contradictory in responses) or (2) diffuse attachments as manifested by indiscriminate sociability with marked inability to exhibit appropriate selective attachments. The unhealthy care producing RAD includes at least one of the following: 1) persistent disregard of the child's basic emotional needs for comfort, stimulation, and affection, 2) persistent disregard of the child's basic physical needs, 3) repeated changes of primary caregiver that prevent formation of stable attachments (e.g., frequent changes in foster care) (APA, 1994). The types of student discussed in this book are often having these kinds of struggles to make healthy and positive connections with care-givers and family situations. They have attachment issues underlying their behavioral problems and may or may not fit into a diagnostic area of RAD. They may also be a poor match or non-traditional fit with typical Conduct Disorder or Oppositional Defiant Disorder clinical labels or with juvenile delinquency categories. While a disrupted home environment or maltreatment certainly does not always equal a diagnosis of attachment disorder or issues, additional consideration of student needs stemming from these experiences is warranted. Attachment problems considered here are physical and emotional symptoms, thinking, and behavior that come from major disruptions in care of basic needs, safety or security, disruptions in early childhood or abusive events.

Five Types of Detachment For Students and Case Examples

Overall, diagnostic categories for attachment disorder or issues include little or nothing from behavior in the school setting and categories do not assist much with school planning or intervention. The types of detached students discussed in this book have school adjustment difficulties stemming from problems with development of basic coping skills, sense of self, sense of safety, and positive connection and relating with others due to disruptions in care giving and lack of a stable environment to foster such basic development. In the school setting, students with attachment issues present some common types of detachment from the more healthy relationships and roles for students. Five major detachments for students include those 1) from themselves, 2) from role of a student, 3) from the peers or staff support systems in the school setting, 4) from a basic effort, 5) from a sense of success within the school setting. These are by no means the only ways that students can be detached from the school environment and process, however these five areas provide common and challenging disconnections for students with attachment issues. Students with attachment issues often have variable emotional, learning, compliance, aggression, social, and relationship functioning at school. Students and families face a broad range of learning, attention, mood, medication, family, placement and permanency issues. These students also tend to have intermittent times of high level instability different from a student with typical Attention Deficit Hyperactivity Disorder or Oppositional Defiant Disorder because problems are often more pervasive and intensified by past loss, disappointment, rejection, sadness, or fear. Some combined and slightly altered school case examples are provided below to show students with a number of attachment, behavioral, emotional, and social issues occurring with a primary emphasis in one of the five detachment areas.

■ Detachment from Self

Jeremy, 2nd grader, White boy, in public school setting had a history of physical abuse and neglect of basic needs with one parent until age 4 and then went to live with the other who had a significant medical condition. Early kindergarten testing results showed functioning in the mild mentally retarded range and he was full of anger, insecurity, fear, and resistance toward school. He was withdrawn, preoccupied with objects and things outside the room, and doing small disruptive actions to keep adult attention. He would unexpectedly lash-out at others and had frequent grunting and growling responses when approached. Eye contact and trust were very low. Sharing at circle time was either minimal or done with monotone voice, showing emotions that did not match the content of his words, and constantly copying others around him with some added exaggerations. When upset he created extreme stories of others being against him and believed others were "bad and mean to him." He fell into replaying past events out of fear and desperation. Jeremy's issues from the past had him detached from an age-typical sense of himself and sense of basic safety at school. This detachment from himself left him unable to share himself genuinely and he disconnected from others. Years of dedicated work from parent, teachers and social work support would result in him advancing up to grade level in many subjects and connecting enough with others to show his mental functioning was really in the average range.

Detachment from Role of Student

Maria, 4th grader, Hispanic girl, in public school and an agency school placement had a history of many residence moves with her mother, brief foster placements due to domestic violence, and mother having serious mental illness problems when Maria was between the ages of 2-8. She had great difficulty accepting any teacher being in charge and had subtle and obvious ways of trying to take control over the classroom. She would complain about whether or not she needed to work, what to work on, the time it took, the method to do lessons and their usefulness. Her arguing and justifying ended up taking major time away from the school day. Eventually, she was placed in a behavioral disorder program. She also had days of unusual behaviors such as angry shutting down, refusing to talk, and going under tables for a long period of time. Maria tracked carefully the feedback given to other students. She commented and involved herself with comparisons to the way staff handled other students' behavior. Unfairness and inequity was on her mind at all times. Maria had many strengths in communication, debating, assertiveness, awareness and tracking but all were being applied to non-student roles with very unproductive results. Once safety and control issues were reduced for Maria, school professionals saw significant underlying anxiousness that gradually increased.

Detachment From Peers and School Support

Alex now in 5th grade, is a White boy with a history of three foster placements and two relative placements before age 6. He also was a victim of physical abuse in the home and was frequently in the protector role with his younger sisters. He struggled to trust adults at school and easily fell into distorted thinking about peers assuming they disliked him, did not want to be his friend, and were going to seriously hurt him over age typical joking or mild teasing. He also turned anger at himself over these difficult times with peers. He was slow to process events at school and was often much harder on himself than school staff. All six home removals were done by social workers and they had taken him to court five times resulting in him being resistant to meetings with school counselors or social workers. When briefly accepted by a group of peers, he would quickly and strongly feel the need to protect them and would engage in physical fights 2-3 times per week on their behalf. This left friends confused and his trips to the principal's office increasing and also concerns from the foster pre-adoptive home as well. Completing the discipline processing was difficult initially and his explanation for why this behavior happened was "I am just a bad kid."

Detachment From Basic Effort

Derell, 8th grader, was an African American boy in public school who had been diagnosed and treated for ADHD (no learning disorders) in early grades and later RAD. He was adopted at age 3 following a termination of parent rights due to neglect and maltreatment. He had limited problems in early grades and had average achievement. With the increased expectations of 4th grade, he intensely resisted school work and refused to cooperate most of the day. Derell complained about writing, obsessed over the exactness of letters and also became intensely down on himself. He escalated with anger and anxiety as he expressed major doubts and worries about the future because of his struggles. He engaged in hourly power struggles given that the focus was on extending basic effort and his stance that "it was all just too much and I can't do it." He clung to the underlying belief that he would not have to do the work if he made it frustrating enough for everyone. When this was not successful, he resorted to extremely hateful and aggressive statements toward staff to push them away. Derell continued to increase the severity of threats and ultimately some violence toward others resulted in removals to the local emergency room. With this detachment from effort, he would drag out homework with parents, not believe he could achieve basic grades and that all assignment work would result in poor performance no matter what. His efforts were mostly toward not being compliant with time schedules or the structure or routine of project activities. His problems in the academic area were clearly tied to emotional and behavioral attachment issues.

Detachment From Sense Of Success

Jaden was an African-American 6th grade girl who attended public school and had been in a number of foster and relative placements between ages 3-10. Both birth parents died when she was between ages 5-7 and she received some emotional abuse while in placement. She carried fears, worries, insecurities, self-doubts, and ambivalence about where to invest her allegiances between her birth family or and pre-adoptive home. She worked hard for periods of time, but then fell into severe doubts that things would not work out for her. She had a good connection with her therapist and foster-mother, but continued to have periods of regression back to behavioral, emotional, and social problems at school. She had sadness over death of parents. She had many struggles at school, but would often withhold effort and have brief 1-2 week major difficulties in grades and citizenship. Set back events for Jaden included being caught giving away prescription medication and being hospitalized twice for suicidal thoughts and hopelessness. Support from school professionals for connection, reassurance, and support was vital to helping her through difficult times. Increasing her connection with consistent school success allowed for better relationship building work at home and in therapy. Her major challenge was believing she could succeed and deserved to succeed in the different areas of her home and school life.

Considerations for Attachment Issues Intervention and Prevention

The major question becomes how to help students who are detached in these five areas 1) become more connected and successful and 2) contain and reduce the amount of stress from the school setting being carried to the home settling. Many attachment interventions emphasize parent inclusion and support as an important part of meeting the child and family needs (James, 1994; Gray, 2003). Research critiques noted good evidence support for beneficial elements of successful approaches for both non-clinical and clinical studies with attachment issues that included being short-term in duration, more focused overall, and goal directed (Bakermans-Kranenburg et a. (2003). Theories that are generally accepted for attachment and trauma issue correction and supported in research included two effective areas of focus: increasing positive quality of relationships with parents and improving stability of environment and functioning (Chaffin et. al, 2006). Researchers in childhood trauma and abuse also recommend placing primary emphasis on establishing a sense of safety through social support and the development of ways to manage fear and anxiety (van der Kolk, 2003). Other summary research literature notes established support for cognitive-behavioral based interventions focused on trauma related issues that include elements of stress management, psychoeducation about reactions of victims, parental participation, and cognitive processing or reframing (Kaufman Report 2004).

Additional conclusions included current field research supporting a helping style or approach to children with attachment problems in a manner that is calm, sensitive, non-threatening, non-intrusive, patient, predictable, and nurturing (Chaffin et. al, 2006). *Why Is Johnny So Detached?* emphasizes incorporation of these critical "how to deliver" issues for intervention that are of equal importance to "what to deliver" issues (assuming interventions are grounded in attachment theory). Incorporating and adapting these prevention and intervention approaches for school issues presents a challenge because students are placed in a variety of classroom or program situations and have other approaches in place already. Information, strategies, and activities from this book can be adapted to a variety of situations to assist school professionals to incorporate an attachment perspective, build relationships and strategies in challenging situations, and also monitor attachment-trauma related symptoms and traits.

The Need For A School Professionals Guide To Attachment Issues

Due to the significant variety of issues presented in the cases described above, there is no basic formula for school professionals to follow for attachment issues at school. This is especially true because individual schools have their own variability of resources, trained staff, class size, and programming availability. A premise of this work is that attachment issues and interference at school is often greater than the sum of separate defiant, withdrawn, depressive, or aggressive parts. Students with attachment issues require extra coordination, sensitive rapport and alliance building, family support, intervention, and prevention work more than isolated issues. Supportive school services face the challenge of increasing knowledge, awareness, skills (adapted and new) to help stabilize and help students with different severity levels of attachment issues being played out at school.

The school setting can be an important place to assist in stabilization for student and family. However, this can be a great challenge as children present a very broad range of biological, psychological, and social issues as well as multiple diagnoses. Tapping into child and family strengths will be enhanced with focused, goal directed, and attachment-trauma specific approach to help individualize and make a positive impact. *Why Is Johnny So Detached?* aims to assist professionals in developing a functional assessment, focused support and skill building interventions. Assessing each student specifically will allow for more informed and realistic expectations which can effectively address current issues with relevant goals for the student and family. This book integrates attachment theory and research to create the following guidelines for working with students with attachment issues. These guidelines include: school professionals and programming working to support student and parent needs; active involvement of parents and caregivers; emphasis on safety and stability; strong communication between school, parents and community providers; school interventions not under-cutting other therapy (or vice versa); reconciling differences in approaches or beliefs; and strategies that consider the severity of attachment issues for each child and family.

How To Use This Book

A School Professional's Guide to Understanding and Helping Students With Attachment Issues can be used as a resource book and it does not have to be used in the exact order presented. It is recommended that professionals should look at all sections to be familiar with the broad range of attachment issues and possible interventions. It can be useful to address specific issues (i.e., negative beliefs or intense fear responses) for a student found to have such problems as a top priority. This book is divided into five major sections: Assessment of Attachment-Trauma Issues At School, Home-School-Community Connection, Student's Sense Of Self and Safety, Student's Perception and Thinking, and Student-Other Action and Reaction Patterns. The assessment of attachment trauma at school section introduces the other four areas, provides more detailed descriptions of issues, and a school functioning assessment tool to assemble information. The other four major sections describe additional attachment issue topics encountered by school professionals. Together each section can advance knowledge, awareness, and skills in working with students and families. Relationships among five major sections and specific attachment issues are discussed. Other information covered in the sections include 1) additional information on specific topics, 2) considerations for the severity of school attachment-trauma issues, 3) general intervention goals, 4) teacher and classroom strategies, and 5) professional-student (and parent) activities with objectives.

This book invites you to build up your professional knowledge, awareness, and skills for working effectively with students with strong detachment tendencies. It can be a base to keep you increasing competencies to effectively connect with the parents and professionals also working with students with attachment issues. There are many challenges working with children with attachment issues and it is especially important to not become discouraged if times are negative for the student and for helping efforts. Those times will occur, but it is adults role-modeling continued commitment and the ways to reconnect and move forward that will make the final difference. Important contributions can be made when professionals work at relationship building approaches that prevent smaller level interference or disastrous declines in student's stability, overall development, and coping.

The four sections describing attachment-trauma issues for students are summarized in Table 1. Each major section, Home-School-Community Connections, Student's Sense Of Self and Safety, Student's Perceptions And Thinking, and Student-Other Actions And Reaction Patterns, has three subcategories of more specific attachment-trauma issues for the school setting.

Limitations and Counter Indications

This book is in not a substitute for a mental health professional evaluation when there are attachment or behavior concerns. This book is not a therapy guide for home attachment issues for students or youth-parent relationships; those issues are better covered in an outpatient clinical setting. It is strongly recommended that if there are diagnostic questions that you refer to professionals who can conduct a specific evaluation for attachment issues and related developmental psychopathology. Applications need to be made within professionals competency and case appropriateness. Some students with intense histories of trauma and attachment disorder disturbance may not be appropriate for some of these types of interventions without thorough clinical consultation and evaluation. These interventions should not be a substitute for school professionals making wise referrals for professional consultation with clinical psychology and social work professionals who are trained in areas of attachment problems or disorder, trauma, abuse, and neglect. Ideally, clinical evaluation and discussion with school professionals will be constructive and produce the most successful outcomes.

The four sections looking at attachment-trauma issues for students are summarized in Table 1. Each major section, Home-School-Community Connections, Student's Sense Of Self and Safety, Student's Perceptions and Thinking, and Student-Other Actions and Reaction Patterns, has three subcategories of more specific attachment-trauma issues for the school setting.

TABLE 1 **Overview of Attachment-Trauma Issues Impacting School Performance**

Home-School-Community Connection

Uncertainty of School/Home Placement Stability

Challenges To Coordination Between Home And School

Variable Support of Outside of School Resources/Therapy

Student's Sense of Self and Safety

Low Sense of Trust, Security, and Safety

Intense Shame and Self-Blame

Energy and Emotional Regulation Problems

Student's Perception and Thinking

Intense Fear Based Responses

Negative Perceptions and Hypervigilance

Negative Thinking and Beliefs

Student-Other Action and Reaction Patterns

Self-defeating Relationships with Peers and Adults

Major Problems with School - Social Engagement

Low Acceptance of School Structure and Rules

Subcategories group together a number of possible weakness or strengths, competencies or deficits for the student dealing with attachment-trauma issues. Further descriptions about the displayed severity level of each subcategory are outlined in table 2 Attachment-Trauma Issues Impacting School – Levels of Severity. These descriptions are a guide for where a student may be functioning currently or they may be fluctuating between some severity levels. In the next section, Assessment of Attachment issues at school, there is a rating scale directly tied to these areas. Students with consistently severe interference scores across a number of attachment areas would often have a diagnoses of a behavior disorder, attachment disorder or post-traumatic stress disorder. More mild or resolved levels of attachment-trauma are also provided to serve as a guide. Table 2 can serve as a common reference point for school professionals looking to complete the School Attachment-Trauma Rating (SATR) (covered next section) or have follow-up discussion.

TABLE 2 **Student Attachment Issues Impacting School — Levels of Severity**

Home School Community Connection				
Issues	**Level 4**	**Level 3**	**Level 2**	**Level 1**
Uncertainty of Placement Stability	Student believes school and/or home placement will likely fail and may make efforts to cause placement failure.	Student questions if adults at home and/or school will reject them. Very frequently requests reassurance.	Occasional questioning about placement stability. Student responds well to reassurance and has a strong sense of wanting placements to work.	Generally feels confident about placement stability without reassurance from others.
Coordination Challenge of Home and School	Major differences and contradictions in learning or discipline approaches between home and school. Communication is minimal and/or contradictory.	Some home and school coordination, but some key differences in approaches and frequent misunderstandings.	Occasional misunderstandings or differences in approaches between home and school. Frequent coordination and appreciation for challenges and efforts.	Regular communication and support coordinated, no splitting, child knows communication is "air tight."
Support from Outside Resources	Lack of needed or appropriate evaluation, therapy, medication or home support services.	Some but not sufficient therapy and service supports in place for student and family. Many challenges to obtain stable services and forward progress.	Containment and some progress being made in therapy and other service supports. Effective communication among resources.	Stability and good support from therapy and service resources. Plans in place for relapse prevention.

Student's Sense of Self and Safety				
Issues	**Level 4**	**Level 3**	**Level 2**	**Level 1**
Low Sense of Trust, Security and Safety	Student has almost no trust of others and feels unsafe and insecure in vast majority of interactions. Views others as being hostile or punitive.	Often very low trust or selective about who to trust. Student views neutral interactions as negative and mildly negative interactions as attacking.	Occasional trust when others provide extra reassurance. Emerging sense of safety and security, but often needing help and reassurance.	Consistent levels of trust and security. Student recognizes own impact on relationships.
Intense Shame and Self-Blame	Pervasive, profound, paralyzing shame in most areas of functioning. Rages and hopeless feelings are common.	Interfering and frequent shame or self-blame responses. Poor or limited reconnecting after conflict.	Occasional interference of shame and self-blame. Student is able to reconnect after conflict with help.	Minimal responses of shame and blame. Most conflicts resolved with minimal help.

Physical and Emotional Regulation Problems	Pervasive and/or intense escalation, over-activity or shutting down/hiding. Almost no coping or calming skills.	Frequent over-activity or shutting down/hiding. Limited coping skills even with help.	Occasional over-activity or shutting down/hiding. Student can sometimes regulate on his/her own or with assistance. Student is building coping skills.	Minimal problems with regulation. Uses coping skills on his/her own or with minimal help.

TABLE 3   **Student Attachment Issues Impacting School — Levels of Severity**

Student's Perception and Thinking

Issues	Level 4	Level 3	Level 2	Level 1
Intense Fear Based Responses	Frequent replay of intense past fear or traumatic events in current relationships with adult and peer. Confirmed or likely flashbacks or dissociation.	Occasional replay of past fear or traumatic events with a limited number of people. Possible flashbacks or dissociation. Some response control for times of triggered fear.	Limited replays past fear or traumatic events at a a low intensity. Mostly stays in the present, but often needs assistance when stressed or experiencing change.	No replays of past fear or traumatic events. Generally present during conflicts or struggles at school. Past seen as the past.
Negative Thinking and Beliefs	Nearly constant, intensely negative distorted thinking and beliefs about self, past, school, or others.	Frequent and strong interference from negative beliefs. Some ability to be neutral or occasionally positive in thinking.	Even mix of positive and negative thinking and beliefs. Mild to moderate distortion. Some pro-social thinking and actions, but often needs help.	Thinking and beliefs are generally based on a realistic view of experience and not distorted from the past.
Negative Perceptions and Hypervigilance	Insistent and persistent negative perceptions of situations. Frequently agitated, hostile, or apathetic. Almost always hypervigilant at school.	Moderate intensity of interfering negative perceptions. Frequent hypervigilance at school.	Mild frequency and intensity of negative perceptions. Occasional hypervigilance and misperceptions when stressed. Corrects them with help.	Minimal distorted negative perceptions and no extremes. Can correct misperceptions with minimal or no help. No interfering hypervigilance.

Student-Other Action and Reaction Patterns

Issues	Level 4	Level 3	Level 2	Level 1
Poor Acceptance of Structure	Almost always challenges structure persistently and intensely. Won't accept much teacher or class rules and seeks inappropriate control.	Many challenges to rules and structure. Seeks control of some select situations or issues with moderate intensity.	Occasional challenges to rules with mild intensity. Often responding consistently to redirection or correction.	Minimal challenges to structure and rules. Accepts rules and structure at near age expectation.
School - Social Engagement	Predominantly antagonistic, detached, or avoidant. Engages in highly inappropriate and disruptive behaviors with intense alliances and vendettas.	Frequently antagonistic or avoidant. Engagement consists of brief collaboration, but more often dissolves into complaints about fairness, inability, and equity.	Occasional antagonistic or avoidant, but able to correct with help. Majority of interactions are cooperative or positive.	Majority of social engagements are positive. No interfering antagonism or avoidance behaviors. Can address most social issues that arise during the day without help.
Self-defeating Peer Patterns	Predominantly negative in most peer relationships. Impulsive, reactive or pre-emptive attacks at others. Intense blaming of others for problems. Very poor boundaries, at risk to be abusive, and prone to major incidents.	Frequent and interfering peer relationship problems. Majority of blame put on others. Only occasional ownership of behaviors with superficial apologies.	Peer problems are occasional with low intensity. With frequent help, student can do well with some peers. Accepts responsibility for actions with help.	Basically successful with the majority of peer group. Responds well to social help from peers or adults. Accepts responsibility for actions most of the time.

Assessment of Attachment-Trauma Issues At School

To evaluate a broad range of possible attachment-trauma related problems and impact in the school setting across Home-School-Community Connection, Student's Sense Of Self And Safety, Student's Perception And Thinking, And Student-Other Action and Reaction Patterns, the *School Attachment-Trauma Rating* (SATR) was developed as a non-standardized issue severity rating scale. Overall, category severity scores are calculated by taking the averages of category items. See the SATR Scoring and Summary Chart for specific procedures. A score indicating an additional referral would be four or more items rated at a "moderate" or "2" level or higher for a child not professionally assessed previously. Whenever in doubt, seek additional consultation. SATR scores provide an overview attachment and past trauma related summary information from the staff's perspective. The SATR helps guide how well an attachment-trauma based approach matches with current school issues. SATR scores assist in setting priorities for sharing information in this book, from other resources, and deciding on use of activities that address specific problem areas.

Additional SATR uses include scores being baseline for comparisons with re-administrations for comparison at meetings, tracking of progress or regress patterns, and a source of feedback to service providers in the community. The SATR can be used to compare with standardized ADHD, or behavioral, or emotional measures. The SATR scores are not a diagnostic measure, but a guide to see the potential of an attachment-trauma problem perspective being beneficial for a case and an indicator of rated issue severity. The Home-School-Community Connection section is intentionally placed as the last section of the SATR after the rater has taken a broad look at possible attachment-trauma related issues under the major categories. Professionals are encouraged to check-in with parents about the SATR results and how to best coordinate available time and approaches at school in order to best support educational and home goals.

SATR

Student Name_____ Age _____ Grade _____

Date: _____   Rating Staff: _____

Time Knowing Student _____ Staff role with student: _____

Please rate the student for the issues below.	Current Problem Level				
Functioning Areas	Severe 4	Major 3	Moderate 2	Low 1	None 0
1. Struggles to have basic trust of others.	4	3	2	1	0
2. Struggles to feel a sense of safety or security.	4	3	2	1	0
3. Reacts with shame to many issues or mild conflicts.	4	3	2	1	0
4. Intense emotional responses suggesting fear or traumatic event interference.	4	3	2	1	0
5. Problems with regulation of energy or activity level. (circle a specific dysregulation tendency: fast paced, slow paced, or fast/slow combination).	4	3	2	1	0
6. Intrusion from past hurtful thoughts or memories.	4	3	2	1	0
7. Strong and interfering negative views toward self, school, or life.	4	3	2	1	0
8. Student fights for control over many issues causing interference in functioning.	4	3	2	1	0
9. Interfering levels of attention seeking from others; acts very "needy".	4	3	2	1	0
10. Problems expressing or identifying feelings.	4	3	2	1	0
11. Over-concern for or excessive focus on unnecessary events in environment or specific actions by others.	4	3	2	1	0
12. Intense or frequent challenging of rules and structure.	4	3	2	1	0
13. Destruction or aggression toward self, others, or property.	4	3	2	1	0
14. Stealing and/or lying problems.	4	3	2	1	0
15. Acts emotionally superficial and/or charming with adults or peers.	4	3	2	1	0
16. Avoids or has limited engagement with individuals or peer group.	4	3	2	1	0
17. Frequent verbal exaggeration in student reporting and/or obvious copying of others to fit in or look special.	4	3	2	1	0
18. Persistent negative actions in peer relationships or socially self-defeating behaviors.	4	3	2	1	0
19. Expresses insecurity about the permanence of school or home placement.	4	3	2	1	0
20. Student has preoccupation with home behaviors problems or family issues creating interference at school.	4	3	2	1	0
21. Student has problems establishing working relationships with school professionals.	4	3	2	1	0
22. School staff has challenges in coordinating expectations, discipline, or educational approaches with home.	4	3	2	1	0
23. Insufficient family support services or therapy for child and family.	4	3	2	1	0

SATR Scoring and Summary Chart

Have teachers or other school professionals complete the SATR.

Professionals should know the student at least 4-6 weeks.

The purpose of the SATR is to track the severity of attachment-trauma issues for ongoing monitoring of progress and needs. Four or more 2 (Moderate ratings) on 1-18 for a student not previously assessed, would suggest needed referral for further assessment. The SATR is not intended or developed for clinical diagnostic purposes. It can be forwarded as summary information to professionals doing therapy or evaluation for the child with parent-guardian release of information.

■ Attachment-Trauma Sections

Self-Security (SS)	1- 5 Total _____ / 5	Average = _____
Perception and Thinking (PT)	6 - 11 Total _____ / 6	Average = _____
Social Action Reactions (SA-R)	12-18 Total _____ / 7	Average = _____
Home-School- Community Connection (HSCC)	19-23 Total _____ / 5	Average = _____

Recording of dates, rater, area averages, and total items scored at 3 & 4 level of problem.

Date	Rater	SS	PT	SA-R	HSCC	3 & 4 total
_____	_____	_____	_____	_____	_____	_____
_____	_____	_____	_____	_____	_____	_____
_____	_____	_____	_____	_____	_____	_____
_____	_____	_____	_____	_____	_____	_____
_____	_____	_____	_____	_____	_____	_____
_____	_____	_____	_____	_____	_____	_____
_____	_____	_____	_____	_____	_____	_____
_____	_____	_____	_____	_____	_____	_____

Home-School-Community Connection

Uncertainty of School/Home Placement Stability

Challenges to Coordination between Home and School

Variable Support of Outside of School Resources/Therapy

This section is first because it represents an important theme that carries through the entire book. School professionals will have their best guide to working with mild or more severe attachment problems at school by having good communication with home and community care providers. With more intense cases, there are often feelings of uncertainty about the stability, appropriateness, effectiveness, and safety of the student's placement in a school classroom or program setting. Frequently, home has stress and attachment issues effecting parent-child relating and there can be concerns about placement stability. It is strongly recommended that if there are diagnostic questions that you make a referral to a professional who can conduct a specific evaluation for emotional-behavior problems, attachment issues and related developmental psychopathology.

With difficult or high volume of problems, coordination and communication become a major challenge. More severe cases may need guidance from parents or caregiver and from qualified professionals working with the child in the community. There will be cases where there is no community or therapy involvement for the child and family. *Why Johnny Is So Detached?* along with other materials can provide a guide to approaches that are sensitive to child and family needs in these situations. Parents and caregivers assume on much of the challenge with children with attachment problems and disorder, therefore schools can help by being supportive and complementary to family and treatment goals. It should be made clear at some point what roles will or will not be helpful from school professional interventions. Much of the time there will be desire for involvement.

All the activities in *Why Johnny is So Detached?* are open to inclusion of parent and care-givers. More severe cases should have parent or caregiver involvement at the start, if possible, to help establish some fundamental comfort and trust. The advantages of having a parent being present with a more severe student include: better clarity about goals and plans, reduced chances of being uninformed or put at odds with each other through misinformation or reports from the child, reduced chance of slow or misguided start, and an opportunity for meaningful feedback and communications. Teacher and classroom strategies and activities are also open to adjustment based on parent input of a student's working style or specific needs. The primary goal of professional actions at school is to support overall student stability and the building of parent-child relationships by reducing school related stress and subsequent negative carry-over to home.

Student's Sense of Self and Safety

Low Sense of Trust, Security and Safety

Intense Shame and Self-Blame

Students with attachment issues often bring to school a more insecure sense of themselves and their environment. Based on past negative experiences with adults, it is common for students to have a high level of distrust about what people say and how they will be treated. Students with attachment issues also tend to have a strong tendency toward self-blame and shame over events that happen in their school life and life in general. This view of self is often an additional part of why they are hesitant or quite resistant to bring themselves to helping relationships or teacher-student relationships. Good ground rules for relationship and alliance building include: 1) be informed about student's background, 2) set ground rules and be consistent, 3) be prepared and goal directed yet be flexible to the needs of the day, 4) remember lower levels of social-emotional age needs and expectations, 5) don't do too much or go beyond appropriate and qualified roles, 6) do not assume very little can be done 7) apply awareness and knowledge and coordinate it with others, 8) seek out support for additional stress that comes up professionally from working with children with attachment issues, and 9) work on physical regulation issues (covered in next subsection).

Some typical student relationship building activities may work if adapted to the student's specific needs. It is best to avoid activities like board games that tend to dominate interaction and become the main focus. Simple interactions and activities (catch, clay work, drawing) allow for the child to express him or herself and bring in more of their thoughts and feelings like shame or distrust that are often underlying. Typical themes to be alert for in early relationship building discussions include: misperceptions of others' statements, intentions, or actions and also unexpected and low threshold triggers for fears, anger, or aggression. Children with attachment issues often have many unmet developmental needs and there are great benefits to not being overly challenging too early in relationship building. Alliance building may need to take place at a younger level than student's chronological age. It is important to establish a focus on specific issues through some activities the student will not find too threatening. Short-term interventions can make a difference with school adjustment even if there are many issues to address. Adults leading by example with hope and belief in creating a different and better educational path is essential. In the cases of Maria and Derell, they were in classrooms that incorporated many small group activities that were at a lower challenge level that would be fun for much younger children. They both had resistance, but also attraction to these activities with balloons, bubbles, finger painting that allowed younger age expressions that were skipped over to a large degree in their early experiences.

General Goals

1. Build a positive working alliance that complements level of need and has clear boundaries for the student.

2. Support safety and sense of security for the student with needed reassurance and reinforcement on a frequent basis.

3. Clarify roles, rules, situations, and coping plans to reduce misperceptions of relationships.

4. Acknowledge and give active feedback for student efforts and challenges to using supports.

5. Bring in helpful approaches from home or therapy.

Classroom/Teacher Strategies:

1. Meet in advance with parents or caregivers about students with attachment-trauma issues. Use the SATR from previous section to look at issues and areas of need when the student is past initial adjustment to placement in class.

2. List the family and school professionals involved in the student's life to establish perspective on the student's school life. (see Activity #2: My School Day).

3. If the student has moved between relative caretakers or foster care homes, making a list of the moves and people involved in their life can be a good foundation for relationship building. Help the student establish an understanding of your interest in their story and how it relates with their school life.

4. Together do a brief assessment of how the student sees their strengths and weaknesses (see Activity #3 Me At School).

5. Reap the benefits of frequent check-ins with students about basic safety, security, worries, fearfulness, or frustration.

   a. Benefits include countering student negative beliefs and assumptions (covered more detail in the next section).

   b. Students may easily assume you don't care, don't want to know, won't understand, cannot help, or are not to be trusted.

c. Trust will have to be built gradually through actions, activities, and interactions. It is not something just stated.

d. It is important to develop a focus, plan, and connection with their home-base.

6. If you see variability in their functioning on different days, evaluate and explore their view of school days with Activity #4 Three Kinds of School Days.

7. It is beneficial to provide additional preparation or review to students individually and in preparation for classroom or small group expectations.

8. Help student show some basic competency or leadership skills in the classroom

9. Recruit extra support and guidance to work on difficult peer relationship problems such as peer helpers or mentors.

 ACTIVITY #1: Catch and Copy

Grades K – 8

Overview Engaging activity that has movement and interaction.

Objectives

1. Assesses interaction tendencies, cooperation and acceptance of adult directions in an interactive way.

2. Allows for interaction to build openness, comfort, and expression.

Procedures

1. Have one or a few indoor balls for catching or rolling.

2. State rules of being safe, working together, and enjoying the activity.

3. Review rules for the activity by randomly throwing the ball in different ways.

4. When the student catches the ball have him/her repeat one of the rules.

5. For younger children roll back and forth to start.

6. Build up to indoor ball catch with some different levels of difficulty.

7. Change the style occasionally and see if the child follows.

8. Challenge each of you to come up with some different ways. Bounce, roll, bat, roll off hand, roll off leg, hand, arm, foot; high one, low one, two handed, one handed, spin, curve, bounce off wall, bounce off knee, foot, head, make up a trick and pass it, eyes closed, or work for 5-10-20-30 toss-catches in a row.

9. Guide excitement level with more structure and slowing of exchanges, commentary and positives for sticking with the rules.

10. Take brief breaks for discussion.

Discussion Questions

1. Have you done something like this before?

2. Did you like to think of new ways of doing things?

3. Did you enjoy the activity?

4. Did you have fun? How come? Do you like to take the lead in games?

Follow-up

Introduce new and different types of types of balls or bean-bags to play catch. Slowly increase difficulty level as appropriate and helpful. Advance by tossing the ball and other person catches with their feet together. Extend to a juggling activity where you toss the ball back and forth going for "no-drop exchanges." Work for a common goal of 5-10-15. Advance with tossing two balls at a time, then cross over toss, or use different types of objects or mixed objects.

 ACTIVITY #2: My School Day

Grades K – 8

Overview Clarifying basic school structure: people, places, and perspective on purpose of school activities.

Objectives

1. Cooperatively creating a reviewable outline of child's environment and school routine.

2. Assess level of awareness and feelings surrounding people, places, and purposes of their day.

Procedures

1. Use the My School Day worksheet.

2. Have the student fill in person, place, and purpose for each time of the day. Include bus rides and transition times. Complete the first three labeled columns. Other columns are for follow-up options later.

3. Provide basic orientation and review their day from beginning to end (mix in discussion and questions).

4. Ask for some descriptions and reactions to people, places and purposes informally.

5. Use open questioning and see what comes up. For example: you may ask their perspective on the obvious lunch room time: What is the purpose of resource room? And you may receive an answer like "to get help with math" or they may say "to get away from all the stupid rules of Mr. T's class, he is just out to ruin my life".

6. Cue in on child's expression and non-verbal communications about issues.

7. Give feedback about their expressions or add some guesses about their thoughts or feelings if they appear to be holding back feelings.

Discussion Questions

1. What do you think about your school day? What is the low point?

2. Who do you look forward to seeing?

3. What is fun or easy about your day? What is difficult? What is confusing? What feels uneasy?

4. Were you feeling a little _____ when listing _____?

Follow-up

Once the basics are completed then the worksheet can be copied as a baseline. The two blank lines on the far right are to later go back (using a copy of original) and add issues like 'stress' and 'worries' to rate where the child is experiencing these feelings. Additional place/person specific ratings can be done for 'calmness' 'energy level'.

Rating scale is **1** = very good, **2** = good, **3** = OK, **4** = problem, **5** = major problem.

My school day Worksheet:

Name: _____   **Date:** _____

Person	Place	Purpose		
_____	_____	_____	1 2 3 4 5	1 2 3 4 5
_____	_____	_____	1 2 3 4 5	1 2 3 4 5
_____	_____	_____	1 2 3 4 5	1 2 3 4 5
_____	_____	_____	1 2 3 4 5	1 2 3 4 5
_____	_____	_____	1 2 3 4 5	1 2 3 4 5
_____	_____	_____	1 2 3 4 5	1 2 3 4 5
_____	_____	_____	1 2 3 4 5	1 2 3 4 5
_____	_____	_____	1 2 3 4 5	1 2 3 4 5
_____	_____	_____	1 2 3 4 5	1 2 3 4 5
_____	_____	_____	1 2 3 4 5	1 2 3 4 5
_____	_____	_____	1 2 3 4 5	1 2 3 4 5

Other information about my day:

_____

_____

_____

ACTIVITY # 3: Me At School

Grades 1-8

Overview Student self-rating to work on cooperatively with adult.

Objectives

1. Establish positive rapport and basic ability to look at self and behaviors.

2. Establish openness and good working relationship.

3. Assess views on strengths and weaknesses for relating, sense of self, thinking, perception, and concern areas.

Procedures

1. Copy the Me At School worksheet.

2. Use colored markers and extra paper.

3. Introduce this activity as something that is done with many kids. Explain that we all have personal strengths and weaknesses.

4. Give personal examples if you feel it will be helpful.

Discussion Questions

1. Did anything surprise you about this activity?

2. How do you feel you are doing overall?

3. If child gave excessively positive ratings: Do you think your teacher would rate you the same in _____ areas?

4. From _____ events do you think they would probably rate you a bit lower and in need of work?

5. Which 3 would you like to see improvement on the most?

Follow-up

Watch for some significant struggles or major issues like negative beliefs about self or tendencies to be superficial or exaggerate.

Me At School Worksheet

Name: _____

Use a check to mark how you think you do at the following things at school.

	Low	OK	Good	Very Good
1. Feeling safe	_____	_____	_____	_____
2. Acting safe	_____	_____	_____	_____
3. Trusting others	_____	_____	_____	_____
4. Sharing feelings	_____	_____	_____	_____
5. Sharing my beliefs	_____	_____	_____	_____
6. Having a good attitude	_____	_____	_____	_____
7. Being happy	_____	_____	_____	_____
8. Using humor	_____	_____	_____	_____
9. Accepting help	_____	_____	_____	_____
10. Being responsible	_____	_____	_____	_____
11. Being respectful	_____	_____	_____	_____
12. Giving full effort	_____	_____	_____	_____
13. Being kind	_____	_____	_____	_____
14. Helping others	_____	_____	_____	_____
15. Finding support	_____	_____	_____	_____
16. Having fun	_____	_____	_____	_____
17. Sharing in a group	_____	_____	_____	_____
18. Using coping skills	_____	_____	_____	_____

Me At School Follow-up Sheet

Name: _____

How do I feel about my current ratings?

_____

_____

Do I think others see me about the same?

_____

_____

What items was I surprised about?

_____

_____

Three areas I want to improve on.

Areas	**What to do differently.**
_____	_____
_____	_____
_____	_____

Three personal strengths I have that I should use more.

Areas	**How to show or use this strength more.**
_____	_____
_____	_____
_____	_____

How motivated am I to improve areas and use my strength areas more?

Write in a number _____

Motivation Level

None	Little	Some	Good	Strong
1	2	3	4	5

ACTIVITY #4 Three kinds of School Days

Grades K – 8

Overview Student drawing or a cooperative drawing of Negative, OK, and Good types of days.

■ Objective

1. To increase expression and openness and gather student's perspective on their days at school.

■ Procedures

1. Copy the Three Kinds of Days Drawings

2. Tell the student to think of events or things that happen on Negative, OK, and Good days.

3. Student draws or is assisted to draw a small scene or symbols that show Negative, OK, and Good days at school.

4. Gather details about thoughts and feelings in some discussion.

5. Proceed to the Three Kinds of Days Worksheet

■ Discussion Questions

1. What goes into a/an _____ day?

2. Which do you have the most of? Second? The least?

3. What kinds of things make a difference in how the day ends up?

4. If a day starts Negative, how can you make it turn around?

5. What are some small things you can do today or tomorrow to make a difference?

6. Who else can help with ideas or support?

7. Are some days a mix of the three kinds of days? Explain?

■ Follow-up

If the child is overwhelmed by this drawing activity then have him/her show you some faces and make up some drawings or list the feelings you see to keep the activity moving.

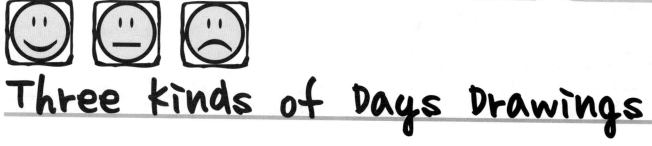

Three kinds of Days Drawings

Name: _____

Good Day: Draw a scene or symbols below that describe a good day for you.

OK Day: Draw a scene or symbols below that describe an O.K. day for you.

Negative Day: Draw a scene or symbols below that describe a bad day for you.

Three kinds of Days Worksheet

Name: _____

What can create a Good day?

_____

_____

What can create an OK day?

_____

_____

What can create a Negative day?

_____

_____

Which do you have the most of? **Good** _____ **OK** _____ **Negative** _____

Are some days a mix of the three kinds of days? Explain?

_____

_____

What kinds of things make a difference in how the day ends up?

_____

_____

If a day starts Negative, how can I turn it around for the better?

_____

_____

What are some small things to do today or tomorrow to make a difference in the kind of days I have?

_____

_____

Who else at school can help with ideas or support?

_____

Energy and Emotional Regulation Problems

Excessive, variable, and interfering levels of physical energy and emotions are common characteristics of youth with attachment problems (Schore, 2003). Current neuroscience research has documented that many children with a history of trauma or abuse can experience an altering of neurological and physiological systems that make them more sensitive to stimuli and more reactive (van der Kolk, 2003). Basic physical energy regulation work may need repeated assistance and efforts in some cases to just contain regulation problems. However, this work is crucial to support student's engagement of their environment and relationships to build more stable thinking and problem-solving competencies. The case example of Jeremey (detachment from self) is a good example of a student with low external energy, but underlying tension and pressure that was quick to explode when triggered. He disliked many relaxation activities and did much better with active movement to increase his energy to engage productively. He needed much practice in basic ways to regulate himself and not get over excited. Jeremey liked to incorporate some fantasy and video game imagery into discussions about calming or relaxing. With his input and creativity he kept more connected with regulation efforts and liked following his mood and worry monitor that was designed for checking-in daily.

Physical regulation is a fundamental issue of focus because it can impede progress in almost all other areas if not addressed. Regulation problems have a close relationship with the student's feelings of insecurity. School professionals should guide the student to define regulation or energy management as cooperative work. Take extra care to avoid the child interpreting such work as "just another thing I do not do right." Essentially, better coping skills or thinking are not likely to occur in students with more intense problems with energy regulation. Many students will need a cooperative coaching approach to learning relaxation and will not be able to initially use self-monitoring approaches, or know when to apply coping skills. Begin activities at a simple and basic level to match the student's emotional and social functioning level. A student may benefit from practice at accurately reading facial expressions while doing relaxation working to help provide a more personal reference point.

If there have been years of poor regulation and/or an additional biological based diagnosis (e.g., fetal alcohol effects or Childhood Onset Bipolar Disorder), then there will likely be years of challenging work to contain or improve regulation abilities. If the student is taking medication, there may be a number of issues with medication effectiveness or side-effects (e.g., tiredness). Close observations about overall regulation issues and especially reactions to different environments and coping efforts will be helpful to prescribing physicians. It is rare that a child with regulation issues will have them resolved simply through medication interventions.

▪ General Goals

1. Establish a focus on physical regulation issues for school environments to help with visible overexcitement and internal tension or fear.

2. Join with parent and student to create helpful physical and mental calming plans and routines for school.

3. Develop and use verbal and visual meters for energy, stress, or anger. Refer back and forth with student's facial expressions.

4. Coordinate and complement home approaches and other therapy.

5. Praise, practice, and give feedback for basic regulation work to establish some initial energy regulation success.

■ Classroom/Teacher Strategies:

1. Gather information from home (Activity #5).

2. Address regulation issues early in the year to avoid escalation to disruption and defiance.

3. Emphasize the importance of ongoing regulation work and actively reinforce regulating plans and basic routines (see Relaxation Progress Sheet).

4. Work to understand the intense internal pressure or tension from attachment or traumatic experience issues and do not assume a calm inner emotional state when there happens to be a calm external appearance.

5. Plan strategic breaks for the student to avoid excess energy or stress build-up.

6. Establish communication between teachers about levels of agitation or stress levels at specific times and learn to apply basic coping skills (see Activities #6, #7).

7. Consider a sensory integration evaluation within school system.

 ACTIVITY #5: Home Ideas For Calming At School

Grades K – 8

Overview Capitalizing on successful calming or grounding activities or objects from home to help at school.

■ Objectives

1. Build positive communications and coordination with home and school.

2. Obtain parent input on helpful transfer assisting actions.

3. Intervene early or in a preventative manner with regulation problems.

■ Procedures

1. Complete SATR and have an idea of the relationship between regulation issues and other primary attachment-trauma problem areas.

2. Set up a meeting with parent by phone or in person.

3. Discuss medication issues (if appropriate) with parent. Have some suggestions ready or some plans on how to assist with regulation building at school.

4. Work to identify past or likely times of stressful events and how to counter and give extra support during those times.

■ Discussion Questions

1. Are there some ways you see physical excitement or energy impacting home (or school in the past if relatively new student)?

2. What helps the child feel more calm and secure at home or at school in the past?

3. What things stir the child on a bad day?

4. What are some warning signs for when you know that this student is having a hard time regulating? Any major events coming up?

5. Would having a picture of parents at school, a familiar object be helpful or calming, but not cause a distraction?

6. What ways can you support good transitions from home to school?

■ Follow-up

This can be good basic information gathering for team meetings or IEP and to pass along to teachers or other staff. Also use a copy of My School Day Worksheet (page 22) and track energy level as one of the items in the far right columns to see the rate levels at different times of the day.

Information Gathering on Student Regulation Issues

School Staff: _____ Date: _____

Student: _____ Grade: _____

Information Source: _____

Ratings on the SATR	SS	PT	SA-R	HSCC	3 & 4 total
	_____	_____	_____	_____	_____

Are there some ways you see physical over-excitement or energy impacting home?

_____

_____

What helps the child feel more calm and secure at home currently or at school in the past?

_____

_____

What things upset the student on a difficult day? Are there problem transitions to or from school?

_____

_____

What are some warning signs that can alert that this student is having a very difficult time regulating energy?

_____

_____

Are there major events each year or that are coming up soon?

_____

_____

Would things like having a picture of parents at school or a familiar object be helpful and not become a distraction and cause interference?

_____

_____

Other Information: _____

_____

Initial Plan: _____

_____

ACTIVITY #6: Breath, Focus, and Balance

Grades K – 8

Overview Assessing and building-up ability to focus and maintain a calm physical state.

■ Objectives

1. Positively working with an adult who leads in basic focus and grounding activity. Increase basic sense of feeling in control of self and engagement with lower challenge activity.

2. Engage child's creative input and interaction with an adult.

■ Procedures

1. Guide in taking some slow deep breaths to relax and feel more calm and do this for 1-3 minutes.

2. Close eyes gently or almost completely.

3. Hold out hand palm up in a flat and still manner.

4. Balance object (easy for their age or coordination, ball, bean bag, small stuffed or squishy toy) for a brief time goal of 10-20 seconds.

5. Gradually build up to higher amounts of time.

6. Increase challenge in different ways as they achieve success. Try back of hand, non-dominant hand, or foot balance.

■ Discussion Questions

1. Was this easy or hard?
2. Did you like increasing the challenge?
3. Do you feel you can focus better than you thought?
4. What helps you focus well?
5. What makes it hard sometimes to focus?

■ Follow-up

Use the Relax and Calming Progress Sheet to track progress in the students efforts. It is possible to transfer this activity to a small group after they are familiar with it meeting individually, build in some positive social goals for the group that they can more easily focus on since they know the activity and will be familiar with it.

"Relaxing" and "Calming" can be taken back to a copy of My School Day Worksheet (page 22) and placed in the blank lines of the two far right columns. You and the student can rate how well they are doing in these areas in specific settings.

ACTIVITY #7: Plastic and Jello

Grades K – 6

Overview Work to assess and build up brief ability to release extra energy.

Objective

1. Assess and build skills and ability to regulate physical energy, focus, to work cooperatively and positively, and to release tension.
2. Build cooperative relating.
3. Have initial success on a joint activity.

Procedures

1. Introduce activity as something done together to check-in on energy and relaxation.
2. Be willing and active in modeling tensing and relaxing, actively acknowledge that we all look a bit silly doing the activity.
3. Uses sports or actor examples of people who use these activities to relax and work at being under control.
4. Coach student to tense their body making a muscle group hard like plastic, one muscle group at a time.
5. Have them knock lightly on arm or leg to test it out.
6. Have the student relax and see how loose or "jello – like" they can make their face, shoulders, left arm, right arm, left leg…
7. Cue the student to increase ability to concentrate and have basic self control.
8. Remind the student about how they can use this to lower their level of tension.
9. Role-play some hypothetical events and how they might use this strategy to calm themselves. Talk in terms of facial expressions to help student become more engaged.
10. Discuss using with other professionals in the school setting.

Discussion Questions

1. Were there some parts difficult to make "jello-like"?
2. What are some times they would likely feel plastic or jello?
3. What are times at school they feel tense or more relaxed?
4. Are their times at school they wished they could switch from being one to the other?
5. What are some other ways their body feels? (draw a picture or have them create good descriptions for follow up)
6. What are other times you have or can use this relaxing activity?

Follow-up

Initiate use of a basic meter for tracking stress and their ability to lower their stress level. More advanced energy, tension, or focus mapping, go through the 1 2 3 4 5 rating sheet or combine with My School Day Worksheet (page 22).

Relax and Calming Progress Sheet

Name: _____

SCHOOL STRESS METER

Calm	Good	OK	Mild Stress	Stressed	Very Stressed
1	2	3	4	5	6

Date	Relaxing Activity	Meter Start	Meter End	Where Practiced
_____	_____	_____	_____	_____

What is helping? _____

What to add? _____

Other times I have or can use this relaxing activity: _____

_____

Date	Relaxing Activity	Meter Start	Meter End	Where Practiced
_____	_____	_____	_____	_____

What is helping? _____

What to add? _____

Other times I have or can use this relaxing activity: _____

_____

_____

Student's Perception and Thinking

Intense Fear Based Responses

Negative Perceptions and Hypervigilance

Traumatic experiences including abuse and neglect often create an overall negative impact on a student's expectations for the future, belief in how actions will achieve results, and the develop of a coherent story about themselves and their life (Siegel, 2003). Students operating from intense fear based responses at school can exhibit behaviors such as tantrums, aggression, tuning out, arguing, stealing, lying, or playing incapable. It is possible that in the past these behaviors were ways to meet some basic needs (emotional or physical) in times of neglect or trauma. A youth's intense fear based mode and problems regulating emotions can frequently be set-off by environmental or internal triggers that tie back to traumatic events (Schore, 2003). Defiant behavior issues are covered later by design, because "trouble-shooting" at that behavioral level too soon in the process runs a risk of missing many underlying causes. It is important to first look at and remember the potential internal thought and belief issues related to fear and trauma responses that are likely driving behaviors. In the case of Jeremy's detachment from self, he was overly caught up in intense fear reactions to consistently interact in a way that developed a sense of self. He perceived that others wanted hurt him, hurt his non-abusive parent, or be mean to him like a past abuser. Communication with the treating therapist was crucial to help school staff, parent, and student address these reoccurring issues. The parent likewise brought suggestions back to school for how to provide reassurance through occasional phone calls and redirection.

Professionals can help students with plans that target lowering the intensity, frequency, duration, and impact of negative perceptions and reactions at school. Also reducing the number of triggers that can be occurring at school which can be simple events or stimuli in their day. Some triggers for Jeremy included going down stairwells, teacher turning lights out, and adult even slightly raising their voice that staff did not think of as threatening, but posed a true perceived threat to him. It is also helpful to assist students in expressing in words or activities the hidden "worst case" perceptions about school that may be thinking in their minds instead of angry or aggressive outbursts. Derell had a number of distorted perceptions about school expectations he was certain he would be unable to meet. Once he was able to state and not act out this intense doubt and helplessness, he was able to consider alternatives and start to see himself in a preparing mode for the future and not viewing each challenge as "I know it was just too hard, why bother at all". Given these negative perceptions, students often are hypervigilant in the environment and are over concerned about unnecessary events or actions around them. Maria was able to engage in activities to reduce her need to monitor adult actions and classroom activities with such hypervigilance. With persistent staff effort in relationship building, worksheet activities and classroom interactions, she was able to see humor and accept playful redirecting when this habit of "over-concern" would interfere.

Stages of student adjustment to the school setting (see Table 3) was developed to outline some of the common levels of overall adjustment. This approach brings an additional view of how the student is functioning beyond levels of attachment-trauma symptoms or trait severity. The lower stages of functioning include Rock Bottom, Raging and Wrecking, and Settling-Unsettling. These lower stages encompass more intense negative thinking and defiant behaviors and very low trust in relationships. The upper three levels have students better able to the slowly move forward through stages of Connecting – Disconnecting, Consistency Experimentation and Establishing, and "Secure Enough" Student. It is useful to keep these stages of school adjustment in mind in addition to considering symptom and trait severity. In the case of Derell (detachment from effort), he had significant time at the lower levels and definitely hit "Rock Bottom" as severe threats continued and hospitalizations occurred because of dangerousness. A change in school placement resulted in an increase therapeutic interaction and support in the school and an outpatient setting. He was able to start anew closer to a Settling-Unsettling level. With the cases of Jaden (detachment from success), she was mostly at the stage of Consistency Experimentation and Establishing over the course of about 12-18 months. For both cases, a continued commitment to looking at the distorted perceptions and working to provide positive experiences helped them achieve a sense of security and perception of the possibilities for them. The basic achievement of students knowing how they would be kept safe or could keep themselves safe made a dramatic difference.

TABLE 3 **Stages of Student Adjustment for Attachment Issues**

Rock Bottom:

Most of the student's attachment-trauma issues are at a high severity level (pgs. 9–10). Students need a containment focus for their most intense issues and subsequent attachment-trauma problem driven events, thinking, reacting, and images. Goals need to be about safety plans, basic containment, understanding cues, simple body regulation, helping basic security and how to head off escalation. Significant consultation is needed with parents/caregivers and treating professionals to help stabilize.

Raging and Wrecking:

Many of the student's attachment-trauma problem issues are at levels 3 and 4. This adjustment stage often has intermittent intentional sabotage out of desperation and distortion. They often replay old issues of rejection and mistreatment from their past. Goals need to focus on reducing intensity, frequency, and duration of negative events. A major team effort is needed to reconnect after negative events and to have also have accountability.

Settling – Unsettling stages:

Most of the student's attachment-trauma problem issues are at levels 2 and 3 (pgs. 9–10) with occasional level 4 characteristics. This stage is likely marked by transitions, multiple changes, recent placement events that stir attachment-trauma problem issues. There are still questions of "are you going to give up on me?" or "can I get you to give up on me?" Overall, it is hard for students to hold it together in multiple settings consistently. There may be reports of improvement in one setting (home or daycare) while having a backward slide in another (school).

Connecting – Disconnecting:

Early time at this stage has attachment-trauma problem issues at levels 2 to 3 while later they will likely be between 1 and 2. It is a mix of new positives and some old negatives. Repetition of this connecting and disconnecting cycle can happen with people and programming. There are often what appear to be unnecessary, unexpected, irrational conflicts and power struggles. This stage is a key time to try work on student's thinking and belief distortions. The student is at risk for falling back on intense fear based beliefs and behaviors. They are experiencing uncertainty because the student has felt let down many times before.

Consistency Experimentation and Establishing:

Most of the student's attachment-trauma problem issues are at levels 2 and 1 (pgs. 9–10). With less interference from attachment-trauma problem issues, a student may start a school placement at this stage. The student is extending more genuine efforts, committing to basic goals, using skills, and accepting recognition from others. Building greater relationship alliance plus strong supporting home or therapy efforts will be helpful and necessary for the student to advance.

"Secure Enough" Student:

All but a few student attachment-trauma issues are at level 1 and a few at level 2. Students are now able to use strengths and abilities more consistently. If they have made a journey up from the lower stages of adjustment, then further support at school may be needed. Continued reinforcement of reflecting, processing, using supports, and engaging in protective activities will be key for ongoing stability.

General Goals

1. Identify interfering negative perceptions in general, from specific time of year, up coming events, or events in current family or previous school experiences.

2. Assess for common fears being intensified by uncommon extent of pressure and a return to "bad things are coming" beliefs.

3. Gather information from parents about possible triggers for negative emotional responses.

4. Reduce hypervigilance interference and disconnection experienced by the student at school from peers, self, teachers as a result of past fear or trauma responses.

5. Increase a genuine sense of placement security and acceptance with current school programming.

Classroom/Teacher Strategies:

1. Discuss with staff student's adjustment stage currently and what direction they seem to be moving. Review a broad range of possible resources that may be needed.

2. Gather information on fears from parents or caregivers (see Activity #8).

3. Gather information on student's perspectives and develop coping plans through Activities #9, #10, #11).

4. Develop many forms of reassurance after initial understanding of the student's thought patterns about school. Define positive helping roles that are non-threatening and maintain needed structure.

5. Give student permission to give you feedback, while also helping them along with expression of feelings or thinking "I wouldn't be surprised if you thought _____." "Other kids I've worked with have felt _____ and it is helpful that I know, because I might not realize that something I said you did not like _____."

6. Aim to use visual cues and clarify feelings and facial expression to avoid miscommunications.

7. Develop creative community building for the student through activities.

ACTIVITY #8 Background on School Fears and Distress

Grades K – 8

Overview Information gathering to help know depth, breadth, and intensity of fear issues at school.

■ Objective

1. Identify possible insecurity, fear, anger triggers that may come from past experiences at schools or earlier life history.

2. Gather a broad base of possible fear increasing factors and also some countering and calming actions implement.

3. Check for common fears being intensified by uncommon extent of pressure and a return to "bad things are coming" beliefs.

■ Procedures

1. Brief phone or in person contact with parent to gather input. Review some functioning and incident information to have an idea of some triggers at school.

2. State clearly the goal is to have school be more aware and knowledgeable about possible upsetting things for the child and how to make them feel more secure at school and function better overall.

■ Discussion Questions

1. What are ways we can be supportive in the school environment?

2. What environments, times of day, of types of interaction might the child find most distressful?

3. If we recognize intense fears or distresses, then what will be a few good things to use?

4. What types of relationship building here at school might be helpful for the student's present experiences with home adjustment and behavior?

5. Would you like us to have a release of information to talk with the therapist about school related issues?

■ Follow-up

Combine with the SATR Checklist (pg. 12) to have some basic overview of student's issues in the classroom. It may also be good to go back and check for additional details or changes to the My School Day Worksheet (pg 22).

Information Gathering on Student Fear or Trauma Issues

School Staff: _____ Date: _____

Student: _____ Grade: _____

Information Source: _____

Previous information from teacher or staff on regulation issues.

Ratings on the SATR	SS	PT	SA-R	HSCC	3 & 4 total
	_____	_____	_____	_____	_____

Are there some ways you see fear, shutting down, or extreme reactions home?

_____

_____

What environments, times of day, types of interaction might the child find most distressful?

_____

_____

What helps the child feel more calm and secure at home currently or at school in the past?

_____

_____

What types of relationship building here at school might be helpful for where the student is at right now with home adjustment and behavior?

_____

_____

What are some warning signs to help us know that this student is having a hard time with fears or negative feelings?

_____

_____

What types ways can help them feel more secure at times of fear or feeling unsafe?

_____

_____

Plan: _____

_____

ACTIVITY #9: Too Super Alert Can Hurt

Grades 2 – 8

Overview Working with excessive focus issues or being caught up in distracting issues or details.

■ Objective

1. Identify, lessen, and eliminate self-defeating over-focus on specific environment or interaction events that interfere with student focus or relationship building.

2. Decrease perceived need and time taken up with hypervigilace.

■ Procedures

1. Copy "Too Super Alert Can Hurt" worksheet.

2. Check to make sure today is not a highly upsetting day to the point where this might add stress or be overwhelming.

3. Use super alter worksheet.

4. Give brief introduction and read the upper left text box together.

5. Start with identifying some things they watch very close. These may be helpful or interfering.

6. Next identify some things they watch super close that then become interfering.

7. Discuss if the watching helps or interferes.

8. Identify what some of their concerns might be and why they watch so close.

9. Work in needed reassurances.

■ Discussion Questions

1. Did you know you were spending that much time at being super alert?

2. What times is it still important or helpful to be super alert?

3. How does your body feel when your brain is on super alert?

4. What plan might help me lower my concern, focus, worry?

Too Super Alert Can Hurt Worksheet

Name: _____

Super Alert——These are times I become caught up in events, people, or parts of my school day and it is not helpful.   Being focused on my reading is a good thing. Being really focused on my friend having a talk with the teacher or really focused on the consequences Suzy received for talking is not going to help me.

Things I feel I need to watch or have the habit of watching **very close** (VC).

VC _____

Things I feel I need to watch or have the habit of watching **super alert** (SA).

SA _____

What plan might help me lower my concern, focus, worry?

1) _____   2) _____

3) _____   4) _____

What will be good about making this change?

_____   _____   _____

_____   _____   _____

Try the plan on _____ (date) and check-in later on _____ (date)

What helped? What did not help? What did I learn? What more can we do?

_____

_____

_____

_____

_____

_____

_____

ACTIVITY #10: Over-done, Not so Fun

Grades 2 – 8

Overview Reducing excessive actions or thinking that interfere.

■ Objective

1. Identify, lessen, and eliminate self-defeating excessive actions or behaviors.

2. Replace and reinforce more helpful and corrective thinking.

■ Procedures

1. Copy the Over-done, Not so Fun worksheet.

2. Generate real examples or possible examples of the over- done actions in the far left column.

3. Can make-up some examples if it is not currently a problem area to still practice the counter thought exercise.

4. Explain how corrective thoughts can help push back against the over-done action.

5. Have them choose one or two of the corrective thoughts and write that number(s) in the "Plan to remember and change" column. Example: " Remember counter thought 3 and 4 when I get over-competing in gym class. Focus on fun and have some laughs."

6. Help student think of ways to remember this corrective thinking and make the changes in their behavior.

■ Discussion Questions

1. What actions do you think you become stuck in "over-done"?

2. What will be good about have less time stuck in being "over-done"?

■ Follow-up

It is helpful to write a few counter thoughts out on a 3x5 card and have them take them with them to keep at their desk or in a folder. Share information with teachers and they can review their counter thought plan prior to certain activities or at the start of the day.

Over-done, Not so Fun Worksheet

Name: _____

1) Write in existing or some possible "Over-Done" areas.

2) Choose one or more Corrective Thoughts to work against the "over-done" actions.

3) Develop plans to remember and make the changes in thinking and action.

Over-Done Areas	Corrective Thoughts	Plan to remember and change
Over-Concern _____ _____ _____	**1.** Not really important	_____ _____ _____
Over-Focus _____ _____ _____	**2.** Not a big deal	_____ _____ _____
Over-Worry _____ _____ _____	**3.** Not my issue	_____ _____ _____
Over-Comparing _____ _____ _____	**4.** Not my job to watch	_____ _____ _____
Over-Competing _____ _____ _____	**5.** Not worth the time and energy. **6.** _____	_____ _____ _____
Over-_____ _____ _____ _____	**7.** _____	_____ _____ _____

ACTIVITY #11: Stormy Times At School

Grades K – 8

Overview Work with student to help see possible schools problems and ways to address them.

■ Objective

1. Increase connection with taking an outside perspective on school difficulties and not just from their internal view.

2. Increase openness and creative-expressive input from the student about their perceptions of their school day.

■ Procedures

1. Copy the Stormy Times Drawing Sheet.

2. Have client draw their version of a storm scene between the upper lines.

3. Assist the student, as needed, and see how much darkness, lightening and threatening this storm appears.

4. Ask the student to draw or describe for adult to draw his or herslef at the bottom of the page underneath the storm.

5. Have student give facial expression examples of the visible feelings and also the feelings deep inside.

6. Write in specific thoughts or statements to self on such days in the cartoon clouds (draw more if needed) .

7. Ask what the child might be thinking about or picturing in their mind on a stormy day.

8. Be ready with ideas to assist with stormy day if student struggles and has limited ideas.

■ Discussion Questions

1. Was this hard to draw?

2. What feelings are part of those days? (add your views on their feelings in needed or helpful)

3. Did it make you feel uneasy to draw out this storm?

4. Who do you think is there to help you on stormy days?

5. Do other people usually know it is a stormy day for you?

6. Did you start thinking of any certain stormy days?

7. What were some other feelings that may have just been on the inside will you, please show me? Show me some more faces that you may have kept inside.

■ Follow-up

Complete the Stormy Times Discussion Worksheet and the Stormy Times Plan Worksheet to do work on the feelings, thoughts, and helpful actions to take for these identified school issues.

© YouthLight

Stormy Times Drawing Sheet

Name: _____

_____

Draw storm scene between lines above

Stormy Times Discussion Sheet

Name: _____

1. Was this hard to draw?

   _____

2. What feelings are part of those days?

   _____

3. Did it make you feel uneasy to draw out this storm?

   _____

4. Who do you think is there to help you on stormy days?

   _____

5. Do other people usually know it is a stormy day for you?

   _____

6. Did you start thinking of any other stormy days?

   _____

7. What were some other feelings that may have just been on the inside with you, please show me?
   Show me some more faces that you may have kept inside.

   _____

Three common types of clouds are Anger, Fear, or Sadness. Do those come around for you? _____

Add them to your picture if you want.

How many times in a week do you feel like this (circle below).

| 1-2 | 3-4 | 5-6 | 7-8 | 8-9 | 10 > |

What might your face look like with the feelings from those three storm clouds?

What people can I receive support from: _____

_____

It would help to make a clear plan for how to use supports and help myself handle stormy days.

Complete the Stormy Times Plan Sheet to make a good plan.

Stormy Times Plan Sheet

Name: _____

Take some of the difficult feelings on stormy days and write them in the blank.

Work together to come up with choices and plans to help things go better.

If I am feeling _____ from stormy times then my choice and plan is to :

   1. _____

   2. _____

   3. _____

If I am feeling _____ from stormy times then my choice and plan is to :

   1. _____

   2. _____

   3. _____

If I am feeling _____ from stormy times then my choice and plan is to :

   1. _____

   2. _____

   3. _____

Times that I used my choices and plans:

What happened: _____

What I did: _____

How well the plan worked: Poorly   **OK**   **Good**   **Great**

What to add to the plan _____

_____

ACTIVITY #12: Umbrella Support Plan

Grades 1 – 8

Overview Follow-up activity to #10 and #11 to help student look ahead and use supports.

■ Objective

1. Helping the student look ahead in his/her school life and not be limited to just reacting to the feelings or events of the day.

2. Empower student planning to use supports and take action for upcoming events in school life.

■ Procedures

1. Copy "Umbrella Support Plan" Worksheet.

2. Discuss the view that it can be a challenge to look ahead and people have to work at developing this skill.

3. What's coming up in the next week, month, or months?

4. Brainstorm about things that can help.

5. Emphasize knowing the names of support people and specifically how to ask for help.

6. On the lines in the umbrella, write in some people, actions or thinking that will help them feel safe and better.

7. Discuss what will help them remember. Use their umbrella plan and write it at the bottom.

■ Discussion Questions

1. What has been challenging so far this year?

2. Did you feel ready for the last (insert event or time frame)?

3. How are you more prepared?

4. What can you want from yourself?

5. What can you expect from others?

■ Follow-up

Check for some negative beliefs that may be underlying fears

"I never do good on field trips, I am always the one who gets caught…"

To provide recognition of using Umbrella supports there are recognition slips for times the student was successful (see Activity #22: Umbrella Plan Success Slips)

Umbrella Support Plan Worksheet

Name: _____

What has been most challenging so far this year? (examples: field trips, recess, homework)

_____

What is coming up in the next week, month, or months that will be challenging?

_____

Are there some possible stormy times that may come up again?

_____

What support can you receive from others or from yourself to be prepared?

_____

On the lines in the umbrella write in
some support people, actions or
thinking that will help you feel
safe and better when you
feel upset on stormy
days at school.

What will help your remember your umbrella support plan?

_____

Negative Thinking and Beliefs

A student with attachment issues often brings to school strong negative beliefs and thinking that develop from intense fear responses. From ongoing maltreatment or neglect there is typically an intensifying of a student's negative thinking patterns about self, school, and others. Children have developed an overall negative set of beliefs about themselves and their lives that are transferred to people and places they encounter and that can be channeled into aggression (Schore, 2003). Frequently, negative beliefs and thoughts are acted out at school through misbehavior or, sometimes, the thoughts are stated directly. Examples of the strongly held negative beliefs from cases of Allan and Maria include: "I hate school," "everything is too hard," "school is a bad place," "teachers treat you mean and give up on you," "kids always treat me bad," "I will give them the hard time they have always given me," "I cannot survive the punishment of home work like other kids can," "I worry staff will expect good days all the time and I don't like that pressure to be good." Activities of expression like #13 and #14 were helpful in having them identify these thoughts as being a barrier in their school day.

To start helping students with negative thinking and beliefs, one should start by increasing school professional's attachment specific awareness, knowledge and interventions. In the case of Allan (detachment from peers and staff support), he was thinking that serious harm would come his way if he did not defend every indication of possible conflict with an aggressive response. He also believed that he could not control his anger because "he was a bad kid and just had too many problems." As with many students, Allan's intense negative beliefs and thinking had a great impact on the stage of adjustment that he moved through in relation to school. In a similar way, Ellen's belief that the teachers should not be in charge and that they were out to make things more difficult for her created many negative interactions and resulted in placement into behavior disordered classrooms. At high levels of severity, it is a challenge to avoid having the student "burn through" classroom and program placements. These were described earlier as the stages of "Rock-Bottom" and "Raging and Wrecking" stage (pg. 39). Referral for outside therapy was helpful for Allan, Jermey, and Derell and provided a place to vent and process family distortions and insecurities. Therapy was needed for family issues and was a buffer to keep the school setting and home setting from getting caught in a cycle of mutual disturbance. Therapy services were important to address some of the driving forces behind the negative thinking. In the face of intense playing out of these thoughts at school, the basics of safety, security, and reassurance issues are an essential starting point.

■ General Goals

1. Recognize and contain the impact of strong negative thinking and beliefs in the school relationships and student functioning.

2. Help all professionals understand the importance of emotional reconnection after problems and become aware that this may be a very new and healing experience for the student.

3. Keep perspective. Initially, even the most positive learning environment will struggle in countering engrained negative perceptions and thinking. Lowering the intensity and frequency is the goal.

4. Find extra activities for interaction and ways to check-in frequently (on adult terms) to reduce build-up of negative beliefs and thinking.

Classroom/Teacher Strategies:

1. Have a parent-caregiver meeting early to help counter and break up some of these thoughts and beliefs before the student settles into their classes for the year.

2. Identify possible negative thoughts with Activity #13 and also #3.

3. Create ways to work with student's intense negative beliefs about their effort, expectations, or insecurities about performance.

    a. Find a unique ability or develop one.

    b. Build confidence and introduce humor into interactions gradually.

    c. Watch for negative responses to compliments. When you recognize a student's good work, switch to commentary about positives they do to avoid emotional and negative behavior recoil.

    d. Consider lower emphasis on academic progress goals in exchange for moving ahead through emotional school barriers.

4. Counter negative thinking with some plans made in Activities #14.

5. Help student move new thoughts and plans into actions and connect with a special role in the class, such as sharing of a talent, common interest, or showing a strength not previously recognized.

6. Work hard to avoid becoming stuck in a student's struggle to connect their thoughts with visible actions or feelings. Based on the student's behavior, take some guesses or describe some of the thoughts you believe are going on about school.

7. Follow-up on activities like Activity #15 Bricks to Balloons, recognize any small ways there has been progress from previous weeks or previous months on these Bricks.

ACTIVITY #13: BRICKS, Beliefs, and Thoughts

Grades 1 – 8

Overview Identifying negative thoughts and beliefs or actions at school.

▪ Objectives

1. Advance ability to identify and address negative thoughts and beliefs about school or school relationships.
2. Advance student-professional interventions with a corrective approach to help counter negative thought-action patterns that are self defeating at school.

▪ Procedures

1. Know some background about the student's thoughts and beliefs related to school.
2. Explain that some of their current struggles or problem-behaviors will come up in discussion, but that they are not in more trouble or supposed to feel bad about them.
3. Normalize how similar issues come up for other students in general and adults too.
4. Explain how BRICKS can be actions or thinking that can create a block between people and build up walls.
5. State that they have the option to draw pictures or write in words to express feelings. You can help or fill in as needed.
6. Student generates and writes BRICKS. Assist them if they need help.
7. Try to make BRICKS specific to the child.
8. Move in and out of BRICKS they may defensive about and those that they are more open about.
9. Provide some feedback on how big, strong, and interfering some BRICKS are compared to others and discuss them.
10. Are they connected with what their parents or teachers sees as the biggest BRICKS in the way at school.

▪ Discussion Questions (on worksheet)

1. How was it to list out these thought and belief BRICKS?
2. What do you think and feel when they see the pile or wall of BRICKS?
3. How many times has the wall been different or not there when they were at school?
4. Will the BRICKS be there forever?
5. How big, strong, and interfering do you see your BRICKS.
6. Are they interested in busting up or tossing out some of the BRICKS? Which ones most of all?
7. Who can help?
8. If the BRICKS were gone, how would things be better?

▪ Follow-up

Compare activity information with SATR scores to see how much they took ownership of staff identified issues. Use BRICKS discussion to set some priorities for topics for the future. Follow-up with Activity #14 What BRICKS Block and BRICK Busting.

BRICKS, Beliefs and Thoughts Worksheet

Name: _____

BRICKS are negative thoughts, beliefs, or even actions about school that block having better relationships.

BRICKS can be used to protect ourselves so that we don't continue to feel hurt or hurt others.

We have identified how these BRICKS work to keep people away or to give protection we think we need. The bricks that we use are things like – running away, hitting someone, name calling, threatening, swearing, yelling, not following expectations, saying things like "I can't" " I won't" … and the list goes on and on. We can use big bricks and little bricks.

Write in some examples of BRICKS you use:

What do you think and feel when you see the pile or wall of BRICKS?

_____

How many times the wall has been different or not there when they were at school?

_____

Will the BRICKS be there forever?

_____

How big, strong, and blocking do you see your BRICKS.

_____

Are you interested in busting up some of the BRICKS?

_____

Who can help you bust your BRICKS?

_____

If the BRICKS were gone, how would things be better?

ACTIVITY #14: What BRICKS Block and BRICK Busting

Grades 1 – 8

Overview Follow-up from BRICK identifying to look at what good things are kept out when the BRICKS block students from good things.

■ Objective

1. Provide an empathetic approach to question these BRICK thoughts and beliefs being allowed to stay around at school.

2. Positive joining with the student in addressing thoughts and beliefs.

■ Procedures

1. Copy of "What BRICKS Block and BRICK busting" worksheet.

2. Identify a time a BRICK was used.

3. Write out some positive things that were blocked or squashed by the BRICK being in the way.

4. Assist the student in thinking of examples.

5. Save time to be able to go on to BRICK busting at the same meeting.

■ Discussion Questions

1. What things do you think the BRICKS blocked out?

2. How did you miss out on some good things?

3. How did the BRICKS not let me show good things from inside of me?

■ Follow-up

Check back over the Activity #3 Me At School and look for some strengths to help student think of ways to counter these negative thoughts and beliefs at school. To provide recognition of busting BRICKS with recognition slips for times the student was successful (see Activity #22 Enjoyment Drawings and Recognition Slips)

What BRICKS Block Worksheet

Name: _____

We have identified what some of the BRICKS are and now we can look at some times the BRICKS were an interference in your day.

Identify a brick that you use, one time when you used it, and what good things it kept away:

BRICK: _____

Situation I used the BRICK in: _____

_____

What Good Things did the BRICK or BRICKS keep away?

_____

Identify a brick that you use, one time when you used it, and what good things it kept away:

BRICK: _____

Situation I used the BRICK in: _____

_____

What Good Things did the BRICK or BRICKS keep away?

_____

Identify a brick that you use, one time when you used it, and what good things it kept away:

BRICK: _____

Situation I used the BRICK in: _____

_____

What Good Things did the BRICK or BRICKS keep away?

_____

Now that you have worked with times BRICKS are around and what the BRICKS block or wreck. Let's GO TO >>>>> BRICK BUSTING <<< and take charge of the situation.

BRICK Busting Worksheet

Name: _____

What could I do to bust these BRICKS up or toss them out of the way?

Helpful actions to take?

_____

_____

_____

_____

Helpful and powerful thinking that can help me break through the BRICKS?

_____

_____

_____

_____

Reasons I want to bust up these BRICKS

_____

_____

_____

_____

How motivated am I to bust up these BRICKS?

Write in a number _____

	Motivation Level			
None	Little	Some	Good	Strong
1	2	3	4	5

ACTIVITY #15: BRICKS into BALLOONS

Grades 1 – 8

Overview Activity to engage student in being able to see and work at transforming negative beliefs and thoughts (BRICKS) into positive beliefs, thoughts, goals, and actions that are more positive (BALLOONS).

■ Objective

1. Create an emphasis and perspective to empower the student to become unstuck from negative views and thinking at school.

2. Visualize possible active steps needed to allow for changes in choice making and good outcomes (BALLOONS).

3. Support and reinforce a mindset of growth and possibility in where a child's has been more fixed and deterministic.

■ Procedures

1. Copy "BRICKS into BALLOONS" worksheet.

2. Write in the BRICK to transform in the left column.

3. Discuss the notion of the BALLOONS being helpful, positive, protective thoughts feelings and actions.

4. Write in the action, change, or acceptance that needs to take place in the Transition Zone.

5. Draw some BALLOONS the student would like to see more of for themselves at school (e.g., fun, friends, trust).

6. Discuss the / Transition Zone / as being the challenge of what actions or choices needed.

7. Discuss the transition might mean accepting some things that are hard to accept. However, using supports around them they can "go for it".

8. Build up the idea that it is hard work transform their BRICKS but it can happen and you'll help them.

■ Discussion Questions

1. Are some of these BALLOONS things that you have wanted for a while.

2. Do you know other students who seem to have some of these BALLOONS?

■ Follow-up

Investigate how some negative thoughts may be impacting classroom responsibility, respect, and actions that are oriented toward better relating with others. Recognition slips are provided for times the student created a good outcome and good feelings were shared (see Activity #22: Busted **BRICK** Slips)

BRICKS into BALLOONS

Name: _____

BRICKS Negatives	TRANSITION ZONE What to change, accept, choose.	BALLOONS Good Outcome

Student-Other Action and Reaction Patterns

Self-Defeating Relationships with Peers and Adults

Low Acceptance of School Structure and Rules

Problems with School and Social Belonging

Self-defeating behaviors typically come from the perceptions, thinking and beliefs noted in earlier sections. The number and intensity of self-defeating patterns can vary for students with attachment issues. Some typical self-defeating patterns or habits can include being superficial in interactions, exaggerating, shutting-down, lying or defiant rule-breaking behaviors in relating to others.

School professionals need to judge the frequency and interference level of these issues that can occur for other students also. It is unusual for the student to become more genuine, honest, or compliant with strictly behavioral consequence or reinforcement approaches. The professional challenges with high volume misbehavior cases like Maria (detachment from role of student) are 1) not to become overwhelmed by negative behaviors when they are at a high intensity and 2) to have school personnel help create relationships and situations where more positive engagement and choices are modeled and assisted. More charitable views and some explorative learning with this defiance and disruption are essential to work constructively and effectively with negative social interaction concerns. With Maria, teachers were consistent with the basic classroom rules and did not allow her do dictate the daily activities. Of equal importance, they were consistently encouraging in their interaction style and worked to anticipate her emotional responses and needs.

Defiant rule breaking can be driven by different or multiple kinds of attachment issues. Often misbehavior and rule breaking serves to protect an insecure sense of self, distorted perception of the world, distorted commitment in thinking, or establish a desired pattern of actions and reactions. Derell's excessive defense of friends was tied to his early life experiences and he needed repeated coaching, correction, re-connection, and support in addition to enforcement of school consequences. Taking a "you choose (insert misbehavior), you pay the price" approach is one option. However, it will likely fall short of addressing a chronic problems of underlying issues with sense of self, security, regulation, misperceptions and distorted thinking that accompany the behavior. Accountability and consequences are needed along with looking at the relationship aspects of misbehaviors. Consideration of attachment issues leaves the option for changing the type of discipline to be more consistent with attachment specific goals.

Working to overcome an approach that only sends the message "you are the problem" is important. The impact on relationship trust should be considered and discussed. The topic of trust is helpful to approach in non-threatening ways and trust is a topic that students with attachment issues will often discuss. This discussion helps advance the connection of thinking more with their feelings and actions. Many students become stuck in "all or nothing" thinking about trust so activities that work with trust as more of a continuum is helpful (see activity #19).

In severe cases, students can have almost constant talking and question asking for reassurance that appears superficial. Such behavior can be viewed as negative attention seeking or trying to control the environment. A student often has competency gaps and limited or no experience at "being real." Jeremy would at times ask the same questions 8-10 times in an hour at first. Teacher re-direction, coaching, and feedback was done keeping a charitable view and focus on his ability to improve is essential. Working to keeping a positive emotional base and empathy geared toward intervention is vital even when some behavioral consequences for rule breaking are involved.

A good perspective on behavior interventions for attachment-trauma students is that strictly behavioral modification approaches (solutions) for complicated biopsychosocial attachment based problems will rarely achieve the needed results. The three major reasons behavior plans don't work well or may even be detrimental without attachment issue considerations for students include: 1) being very stuck a intense fear based mode and trauma responses, 2) having advanced or pervasive mistrust and/or shame resulting in student not wanting any success and likely the opposite, 3) having intense external or internal regulation problems that drive distorted thinking and actions and undermine basic plan engagement. Some common and general approaches to take toward misbehaviors include:

- Give no or very limited second chances or warnings at school.

- Provide absolute consistency from educational team members.

- Limit and eliminate dramatic displays, tantrums, arguing in front of peers or in the classroom.

- Do not entertain "what did you say?" questions or daydreaming as a way to undermine adults being in charge or to have staff look silly.

- Do not rely on student delivery of important communications until you have built up strong trust and consistency.

- Work to show that communication and relationships have value and yield good results instead of behavior management systems and object reinforcements.

- Make sure there is agreement before being more attachment specific with interventions or prevention.

- Consider student's stage of adjustment (pg. 39) in planning. Consider their stage of progress or regression to help track how they are adapting to the school environment.

- Maintain basic and repeated focus on respect, responsibility, and constructive thinking.
- Identify and target negative thinking and beliefs of the student.

General Goals

1. Improve student's ability to be more genuine with peers and adults in classroom by telling true stories, giving examples from home, comparing less to other students, and consistently establish basic satisfaction in personal sharing.

2. Improve student acceptance of peer and adult feedback about what it means to belong as a class member, playmate, or friend.

3. Reduce student's struggle with belonging or fitting in. Decrease exaggerated behavior that is interfering with healthy peer relating and having trust from adults and peers. Decrease frequency and intensity of lying.

4. Increase consistency of acceptance for basic school and classroom rules.

5. Avoid student playing or replaying the past relationship conflicts that led to intense negative beliefs which impact current school relationships and environment.

6. Create different and helpful ways for the child to re-connect after a misbehavior to avoid a "shame land-slide."

7. Avoid having extended time elapse before creating some reconnection with the student.

8. Coordinate natural consequences for misbehavior with parents and caregivers.

Classroom/Teacher Strategies:

1. Provide student with group time assistance to bring in appropriate things they can share from activity and assist student in being more genuine and truthful in their interactions. Work on Activity #16 to advance toward fully honest and real reporting at school.

2. Give "glowing" acknowledgement of things known to be real and shared more genuinely.

3. Help student to see that what is true and real about them shines and receives attention.

4. Assist student in exploring the patterns and effects of exaggerating or controlling behaviors (see activity #17, #18).

5. Establish helpful and healthy discussion and reflection on issues of trust building (see activity #19).

6. Incorporate ideas listed under general approaches in this chapter.

ACTIVITY #16: Things About Me

Grades K – 6

Overview Assistance for younger and lower social skill children with attachment issues.

■ Objectives

1. Help child move beyond repetitive, untrue, or exaggerated sharing about themselves.

2. Decrease the costs of negative social behaviors and build understanding of appropriate content and amounts of sharing.

3. Involve parents or caregivers if necessary to correct this lack of information or misinformation.

4. Send message to the child that you are important enough for us to really know you and real things about you.

■ Procedures

1. Obtain parent input and involvement if this appears to be an interfering problem.

2. Explain that instead of checking if a lot of things are true or not, set up a plan for specific things to share from home about a day or life events.

3. Preparation for this and assistance can be important especially if there are learning deficits or other psychiatric issues (pervasive developmental disorder traits or disorders in addition to attachment problems).

4. Notify parent of the sheet coming home.

■ Discussion Questions

1. What felt good about building-up more things to share with others?

2. Anything that does not feel good about sharing at school?

3. What would be some more things you would like to share with others?

■ Follow-up

Build a book of these sheets and keep track of things shared to look back over. Also add some drawings or pictures.

Things To Share about Me Worksheet.

Student Name: _____

Dear Parent or Guardian:

We would like you to write down some events from the last week and some unique things about each student to then share at school. Please add some details to help the student remember good things to share about the events.

Things from the last week at home.

_____

_____

_____

_____

Unique things about me.

_____

_____

_____

_____

Things I am excited about coming up in the next 1-2 months.

_____

_____

_____

_____

ACTIVITY #17: Ready, Set, Go Real

Grades 2 – 8

Overview Role-play activity to play out the difference between what would be clearly fake and what would be real.

■ Objective

1. Help distinguish between fake and real actions.

2. Work to build up ways to monitor self and also observe others more.

3. Make issues less secretive or full of avoidance.

4. Communicate that we work on basics to help you be successful and that you are not alone in working on these issues.

■ Procedures

1. Use copy of Ready, Set, Go Real Worksheet.

2. Have them think of recent events.

3. Now think of ways you could change or add to them to make some of them untrue or exaggerated

4. Have them write or tell you them one column at a time and not say which is true or false.

5. Complete the follow-up questions.

■ Discussion Questions

1. Can people tell when we are fake?

2. What comes up that makes people want to sometimes be fake at school?

3. How come being true and real is a better way to go?

4. Have you fallen into exaggerating or making up fake events sometimes?

■ Follow-up

If a lower level of severity and good stability, they may do well with this as a small group activity.

Ready, Set, Go Real Worksheet

Name: _____

Think of some recent events. Now think of ways you could change or add to them to make some of them untrue or exaggerated. In one column below put true events and in the other put in false events (don't say which is which yet)

_____   _____

_____   _____

_____   _____

_____   _____

_____   _____

_____   _____

Can people tell when we are faking?

_____

_____

What happens that causes people to want to tell fake events at school?

_____

_____

How come being true and real is a better way to go?

_____

_____

Reasons I have to be more truthful?

_____

_____

_____

ACTIVITY #18: Puffer Fish Faking

Grades K – 8

Overview Establish cooperative work to increase more genuine relating with peers and adults at school.

■ Objective

1. Increase awareness about how true stories and true feelings are more effective and well received than fake.

2. Help students be more comfortable with sharing of themselves and their experiences.

3. Give peer feedback about what it means to belong to the group as a class member, playmate, and friend.

4. Increase school professional recognitions through commentary like "I liked you sharing your personal story" We can see what you and your life is like..

■ Procedures

1. Use "Puffer Fish Worksheet".

2. Discuss what the small fish would be like to be out in the ocean with lots of bigger fish who might eat them.

3. Discuss the special ability of the puffer fish can blow-up and look bigger to fake-out other fish and keep them away.

4. Explain how this is helpful for survival but not good to do all the time.

5. Be ready to give examples of the other types of faking and guide discussion and examples over to those that are a good match with the student.

■ Discussion Questions

1. Are there times you wish you could puff up like a puffer fish and be bigger than you are?

2. What would you want to fool people about.

3. What would be some examples of when students would do this?

4. What do you think is going on with someone who does this?

5. What could help them break this habit? Why would it be a good habit to break?

6. Are there other ways that students can try to fake-out others with the way they act?

7. Like extra sweet and overly nice?

Puffer Fish Worksheet

Name: _____

Some fish have the ability to puff up when they are faced with danger. Students may also choose to puff up big with words or with acting in ways that are not how they really are.

What would be some examples of when students would do this?

_____

_____

What do you think is going on with someone who does this?

_____

_____

What could help them break this habit? Why would it be a good habit to break?

_____

_____

Are there other ways that students can try to fake-out others with the way they act?

_____

_____

Like extra sweet and overly nice?

_____

_____

_____

ACTIVITY #19: Trust Activities

Grades K – 8

Overview Establish a perspective of working on the trust issues that is behind many misbehaviors or lying.

■ Objective

1. Increase awareness about the importance of trust.

2. Establish a changing and fluctuating view on trust rather than an all or nothing view.

■ Procedures

1. Use the trust activities sheet.

2. Explore their views and beliefs on trust.

3. Introduce the idea of trusting as being something that is based on events (positive and negative).

4. We have the right to decide how much we want to trust.

5. Kids and adults can also give up on trusting anyone at all and this can be very sad.

6. Trust is needed to have the good things go back and forth between people.

7. Talk about how the child is currently being trusted by the teachers

■ Discussion Questions

1. Are there times you wish you could puff up like a puffer fish and be bigger that you are or fool people at school?

2. What would you want to fool people about.

3. What are some people and things you have very little trust for?

4. What are some of these?

5. What are some things at school you would like to be building up more trust for?

6. What would be good about you building up more trust?

7. Is it helpful and/or difficult to look at trust being on a range?

8. What are some ways people build trust with you?

Trust Worksheet

Name: _____

How do you look at trust or think it works?

It is like "you see it or you don't?"

People who are good to you and take care of you are people you can trust a good amount.

A useful way we will look at trust in this book is to have it go from 1 to 5 on a trust scale. Trust can go up and it can go down.

Trust Range

0	**1**	**2**	**3**	**4**	**5**
None	Little	OK	Good	Strong	Total

How much do you trust:

The weather _____   School Lunch _____   Best Friend _____

Other Students _____   Current teacher _____   Counselor _____

Closest Friends (list them) _____

- Trust is something we may earn or loose from others.
- Trust is something others may build up or have go down with us.

What are some things at school you would like to be building up more trust for?

_____

What would be good about you building up more trust?

_____

Three goals to increase my trust. From _____ to _____ , with _____ .

From _____ to _____ , with _____ . From _____ to _____ with _____ .

Check back on success later!!

Problems with School and Social Belonging/Enjoyment

Experiencing a sense of belonging and enjoyment is an especially relative phrase for students with attachment issues. It is important to check how student's view of enjoyment overall and at school. Working on the many attachment areas and subcategories leading up to this section helps the student have a better sense of belonging and enjoyment at school. Enjoyment can be pushed out for students due to a vast majority of time and interaction caught up in the high volume problems. There can be a major impasse to produce positive experiences of enjoyment at school with the combination of the students' basic negative beliefs about their lives and their limited experience with their actions being helpful. School professionals can provide support and assistance as well as solicit guidance from home. School can focus on ways to increase the quantity of enjoyable events in addition to the amount of positive emotional connections at school.

There is often a question of whether children with attachment issues will benefit or handle peer group involvement in the classroom or extra group skill-building sessions. Higher levels of problems will need a careful consideration and team consensus about what is most appropriate. Children with lower level issues and their care-givers have good support can often benefit from group involvement with planned goals. In case examples of Jaden (detachment from success) and Jermey (detachment from self) both struggled significantly in peer group interactions. School counselors and teachers carefully selected fellow group members and kept numbers small. Activities were at a lower level of challenge and simple which greatly increased initial engagement with the activities and lower resistance. Expectations were adjusted when they had more difficult days. Both had staffing ratios that allowed for individual processing and support when needed which helped reduce their tendency to act up to get desired attention. Derell also struggled with peers even after reducing his intense battles over providing basic effort. He needed significant basic rehearsal, preparation of basic statements, and practice to handle conflicts, but eventually grew to establish some good basic social skills. Recognition of Alex (detachment from peers and social support) being in the difficult process of termination of parental rights was helpful and extra support at school was given. Derell's adjustment after his adoption was finalized was accelerated with the communication efforts and guidance done along the way.

▪ General Goals

1. Bring together attachment specific approaches and activities to build peer relationships in unique and lasting ways.

2. Assess some basic skills and strengths to build upon.

3. Increase activity and success of social interaction.

4. Create opportunities for social success by making sure developmental challenge does not exceed child's abilities.

5. Reduce and eliminate disbeliefs or mistrust of basic enjoyment of school and people.

6. Keep perspective that strong negative beliefs may mix with enjoyment.

Classroom/Teacher Strategies:

1. Use additional routines and be prepared for a range of reactions to others having enjoyment.

2. Check on ways to advance any strengths identified in earlier activity #3 Me At School, or activity #11 Stormy Times Plan Sheet). Build plans for them to feel at ease around others.

3. Assess, address, and correct the social roles students take on (see activity #20).

4. Gradually build engagement with segments of enjoyable activities and increase this capability. Build from strengths and create a plan with activity #21.

5. Creatively extend making invitations for highly disengaged students participate. Minimize students making major distractions in defiance and detracting from the enjoyment of others.

6. Encourage hands-on activities over discussions about enjoyment.

7. Keep track of triggers or negative responses to activities and work to create a quick reconnection.

8. Maintain higher structure and supervision over social interaction until trust is built and it's not needed.

9. Role play conflicts outside the conflict moments in addition to addressing some conflicts in the moment.

10. Carefully select peers for some small group activities or adapt a group activity to build success.

ACTIVITY #20: Roles to Play or Not

Grades 1 – 8

Overview Help student with identifying helpful roles to play in peer relations.

■ Objectives

1. Increase awareness about the importance of helpful vs. unhelpful roles.

2. Build awareness and plans to eliminate or change self-defeating roles and actions with peers.

■ Procedures

1. Use the Roles to Play or Not activities sheet.

2. Know ahead some different roles you would like to see them become aware of and look to change.

3. Explore their views and beliefs about different roles shown in peer relationships and friendships.

4. Help define and give personal or possible examples of each role.

5. Discuss and help decide whether to keep, toss away, or change roles.

6. Role-play some examples of the roles given or ones you write into open spaces.

7. Write out short plan to take action on in the next 1-2 days.

8. Question the benefits or unhealthy roles they remain committed to keeping.

■ Discussion Questions

1. Can you think of other types of roles you play with peers?

2. How did you start doing so much of _____ role?

3. Do peers act in these roles toward you?

4. How can I choose more helpful roles with peers in the next few days?

5. How can we know when a role is helping or not?

Roles to Play or Not Worksheet

Name: _____

We all play different roles in families and with friends. Some are helpful and some are not. Discuss how you may play some of the following roles and decide if you would like to keep, toss, or change them some. Last, make a plan for how to follow through on your decision.

Role	Decision	Plan For This Role
Helper	Keep/Toss/Change	_____
Caretaker	Keep/Toss/Change	_____
Defender	Keep/Toss/Change	_____
Enemy	Keep/Toss/Change	_____
Controller	Keep/Toss/Change	_____
Leader	Keep/Toss/Change	_____
Avenger	Keep/Toss/Change	_____
Protector	Keep/Toss/Change	_____
_____	Keep/Toss/Change	_____
_____	Keep/Toss/Change	_____

Other thoughts on roles played with peers.

_____

_____

Do peers act in these roles toward you?

_____

_____

Follow-up: How did my plan to take keep, toss, or drop work?

_____

_____

ACTIVITY #21: Ready for Group

Grades 1 – 8

Overview Help student prepare for improved and positive group interaction.

Objectives

1. Increase awareness about helpful actions to prepare for group.

2. Build awareness and ability to reflect on strengths and weaknesses.

3. Help forecast issues and not be surprised or as overtaken with high energy, competing, comparing, worrying etc.

Procedures

1. Use the Ready For Group worksheet.

2. Explore their views on group interaction they have at school.

3. Assess comfort levels, helping actions, and barriers.

4. Discuss and list strengths.

5. How can they make sure to bring them to group.

6. Think of what helps them feel comfortable in group.

7. What are some barriers to feeling comfortable or OK.

8. Create a plan for asking for a break or asking for help if needed.

Discussion Questions

1. How confident do you feel in your plan?

2. Are there things you have done outside of school that have help you do well in a group?

3. What else might help?

Ready For Group Worksheet

Name: _____

Groups can be a challenge to be involved in. They can also be a lot of fun.

Working with others is a life long skill that can be improved on over the years.

What strengths or positives do I bring to a group?

_____

_____

How can I be more certain that I am ready to bring my strengths and use them well?

_____

_____

What helps me feel prepared and comfortable in a group?

_____

_____

What can throw me off (e.g., upset I am not the leader, frustrated with others) that I can be ready for?

_____

_____

How I will ask for a break or help if needed?

_____

_____

Are there other concerns or issues?

_____

_____

ACTIVITY #22: Enjoyment Drawings and Recognition Slips

Grades 1 – 8

Overview Work on a sense of enjoyment through expression and recognition.

▧ Objectives

1. Help advance a sense of enjoyment and growth in this area.
2. Build awareness and ability to reflect on some skills students have developed through previous activities or hard work on their own.
3. Help establish and affirm progress on how students have adapted some new thoughts, beliefs, actions at school and in relationships.

▧ Procedures

1. Copy of Enjoyment Drawing Worksheet and Recognition Slips.
2. Have student think of enjoyable and fun times at school.
3. Together or separate draw symbols or scenes from these events.
4. Complete discussion questions about skills.
5. Review some previous activities and plan some skills, actions, choices to reinforce. Also give feedback and praise for effort and/or work well done.
6. Complete some recognition slips or have others do so and give them to the student.
7. Check their interest in working for some more slips.
8. Fill some out together if they have recall of some good application of their skills.
9. Avoid making external deals for reward if they have a history of excessive focus on external rewards or distress over achievement.

▧ Discussion Questions

1. What helped this event or events be enjoyable?
2. What did you do differently to help it be enjoyable?
3. What did your face look like? Did that match feelings on the inside?
4. What did others faces look like? What do you guess they were feeling?
5. What skills did I use to help these times be enjoyable and fun?
6. Were there actions or choices I made from previous work that I used to help these events?

▧ Follow-up

School professionals can note some good applications of skills and coping behaviors by the child and give them some recognitions slips. Again, these do not need to be tied to any object reinforcement. The message is, "you are working hard, we see that, we want to recognize and celebrate that work".

Enjoyment Drawings Worksheet

Name: _____

In the space below draw an event or a few events that have been fun and enjoyable at school.

What skills did I use to help these times be enjoyable and fun?

_____   _____   _____   _____

Were there actions or choices I made from previous work that I used to help these events?

_____

_____

_____

Umbrella Plan Success Slip

Umbrella Plan Success Slip

Recognition To: _____

Umbrella plan I used _____

What helped me remember? _____

What were the benefits? _____

Place _____

Date _____

Recognition From: _____

Umbrella Plan Success Slip

Recognition To: _____

Umbrella plan I used _____

What helped me remember? _____

What were the benefits? _____

Place _____

Date _____

Recognition From: _____

Umbrella Plan Success Slip

Recognition To: _____

Umbrella plan I used _____

What helped me remember? _____

What were the benefits? _____

Place _____

Date _____

Recognition From: _____

Busted BRICK Slips

Busted BRICK Slip

Recognition To: _____

BRICK I busted up _____

What helped the Busting? _____

What helped and benefits? _____

Place _____

Date _____

Recognition From: _____

Busted BRICK Slip

Recognition To: _____

BRICK I busted up _____

What helped the Busting? _____

What helped and benefits? _____

Place _____

Date _____

Recognition From: _____

Busted BRICK Slip

Recognition To: _____

BRICK I busted up _____

What helped the Busting? _____

What helped and benefits? _____

Place _____

Date _____

Recognition From: _____

BRICK to BALLOON slips.

Good Outcome

Recognition To: _____

With Who? _____

What Helped It Happen? _____

Place _____

Date _____

Recognition From: _____

Good Feelings Shared

Recognition To: _____

With Who? _____

What Helped It Happen? _____

Place _____

Date _____

Recognition From: _____

Good Feelings Shared

Recognition To: _____

With Who? _____

What Helped It Happen? _____

Place _____

Date _____

Recognition From: _____

References

American Psychiatric Association. (2000). Diagnositc And Statistaical Manual Of Mental Disorders (4th ed.). Washington, DC: Author.

Bakermans-Kranenburg, M.J., van Ijzendoorn, M.H., & Juffer, F. (2003). Less is more: Meta-analysis of sensitivity and attachment interventions in early childhood. *Psychological Bulletin*, 129, 195-215.

Chadwick Center for Children and Families. (2004.) *Closing the quality chasm in child abuse treatment: Identifying and disseminating best practices.* San Diego, CA: Author.

Chaffin, M., Hanson, R.,Saunders, B.E., Nichols, T.,Barnett, D., Zeanah, C., Berliner., L., Egland, B., Newman, E., Lyon, T., LeTourneau, E., Miller-Perrin, C. (2006). Report of the APSAC Task Force on Attachment Therapy, Reactive Attachment Disorder, and Attachment Problems. *Child Maltreatment*, 11 (1). P 76-89.

Child Welfare Information Gateway (2005). U.S. Department of Health and Human Services, Administration for Children and Families, Administration on Children, Youth and Families, Children's Bureau, HYPERLINK "http://www.acf.hhs.gov/programs/cb" www.acf.hhs.gov/programs/cb

Child Maltreatment (2004) U.S. Department of Health and Human Services, Administration for Children and Families, Administration on Children, Youth and Families, Children's Bureau, HYPERLINK "http://www.acf.hhs.gov/programs/cb" www.acf.hhs.gov/programs/cb

Gray, D.D. (2002). *Attaching in Adoption: Practical Tools for Today's Parents.* Perspectives Press, Inc. Indianapolis Indiana.

Hesse, E., Main, M., Abrams, K.Y., Rifkin, A. (2003). Unresolved States Regarding Loss or Abuse Can Have "Second-Geration" Effects: Disorganization, Role Inversion, and Frightening Ideation in the Offspring of Traumatized, Non-Maltreating Parents. In Solomon, M.F. (Ed.) and Siegel, D.J. (2003). *Healing Trauma: Attachment-trauma, Mind, Body, and Brain.* W. W. Norton and Company Inc. New York, New York. pp 57-106

James, B. (1994). Handbook for treatment of attachment-trauma problems in children. Free Press. New York, NY.

Jernberg, A.M. and Booth, P.B. (1999). *Helping Parents and Children Build Better Relationships Through Attachment Based Play,* Second Edition   Jossey-Bass. San Francisco.

Shore, A. N. (2003). Early Relational Trauma, Disorganized Attachment, and the Development of a Predisposition to Violence. In Solomon, M.F. (Ed.) and Siegel, D.J. (2003). *Healing Trauma: Attachment-trauma, Mind, Body, and Brain.* W W Norton and Company Inc. New York, New York. pp 1-56

Siegel, D. J. (2003). An Interpersonal Neurobiology of Psychotherapy: The Developing Mind and the Resolution of Trauma. In Solomon, M.F. (Ed.) and Siegel, D.J. (2003). *Healing Trauma: Attachment-trauma, Mind, Body, and Brain.* W W Norton and Company Inc. New York, New York. Pp1-56.

Siegel, D.J. and Hartzell, M. (2003). *Parenting from the Inside Out.* Penguin Group Inc.

van der Kolk (2003). Posttraumatic Stress Disorder and the Nature of Trauma. In Solomon, M.F. (Ed.) and Siegel, D.J. (2003). *Healing Trauma: Attachment-trauma, Mind, Body, and Brain.* W W Norton and Company Inc. New York, New York. pp 168-195

For additional information *Why is Johnny So Detached?* A School Professional's Guide to Understanding and Helping Students With Attachment Issues, see the website supporting this book.

www.school-attachment-trauma.com

Information at www.school-attachment-trauma.com includes:

Postings of professional feedback and applications of strategies and activities from *Why Is Johnny So Detached? A School Professional's Guide to Understanding and Helping Students With Attachment Issues.*

Additional information about approaches at school for attachment and trauma issues.

Links to attachment and trauma therapy and research websites.

Communications about current and future needs for children with attachment issues at school.

For more information, contact Dr. Ottavi at tmottavi@yousq.net